The Weeleys Horticultural Society
hold it's
AGM
and Social Evening with
Darryl Ashton
Blackpool's Stand-up Comedy Poet on
Thursday
December 10th
At the
Thornton Little Theatre
Four Lane Ends, Thornton.
Starts 7.30 Prompt

Poet to amaze Britain's Got Talent judges

CHEEKY Darryl Ashton

A PROLIFIC poet, author and public speaker will get the chance to show off his skills time before he travels to audition before the Britain's Got Talent judges.

Darryl Ashton, whose rhymes regularly grace the letters page of the Observer, was spotted by talent scouts after reading his works to 50 veterans in Blackpool.

Darryl, 65, who is originally from Great Harwood, was first thrilled with the interest.

He said: "I just got down to my poem for only two minutes and I read three I wrote and performed comedy poems.

"They very politely asked me if I could read my further.

"I read my poem called Cheeky Bum and the whole place nearly fell about laughing.

back to audition in front of the judges in January.

He read Cheeky Bum, of his own view and explained he penned it after hearing a woman ask her boyfriend 'does my bum look big in this?' in Marks and Spencer.

He said: "I read three poems and told them a joke and they said I was quite a character. It's been a heck of an experience and I hope it continues."

And the good news doesn't stop there for the author and satirist as he recently landed a contract to publish his new book My World of Poems, copies of which have even been ordered by Buckingham Palace.

Darryl added: "How many budding poets can claim they sold their books to Her Majesty The Queen?"

Cheeky Bum

You say your rear big or small?' you ask.
'Of course not' I declare,
'I bet your bum looks just the same in everything you wear.'

Oops! That's not what I meant to say.
However far, far I flee,
I don't mean to say it's big for my rear from's behind her

It's probably the fact I've seen.
And I've seen a few!
Oops! I didn't mean I've studied them,
I meant mentioned with you.

I wouldn't look at other bums.
I love my wife,
Your bum is all I'd ever need.
It's sent from heaven above.

You're obsessed with bums — you other beauts.
Most of the stuff I can't...
I don't think I can turn this one...
I'm off now for my own.
Darryl Ashton

My Amazing World of Poems

And Political Satire

Darryl Ashton

Copyright © 2016 Darryl Ashton

All rights reserved.

ISBN-13: 978-1533302601
ISBN-10:153330260X

About the Author...Darryl Ashton:

Darryl Ashton is now medically retired, but he was a silver service Restaurant Manager where his skills took him to land a job on the QE2. He is single, and has no children - well, none that he knows about!

He is a very keen writer, mainly of poetry, covering all kinds of topics; including, humour and more serious writings too. He thrives on political satire, and is equipped with a fantastic, and very wicked sense of humour matched with an incredible imagination.

Darryl also does stand-up comedy poem performances and is involved with various charity work. At one time, he raised an incredible £50,000 just by reading his own poems. His poems have also won several major competitions and he is also a leading reader of poems at various poetry groups on the Fylde Coast, Blackpool, Cleveleys and Lytham, all in the sunny and very friendly borough of Lancashire.

Darryl is originally from Great Harwood, a little town on the border with Accrington and Blackburn. He is a keen teller of jokes, and writing just about anything that takes his interest. Darryl says he's a late starter - he has been writing his poetry for only five years! And he's only just got to grips with his computer.

One really surprising thing that happened to Darryl was receiving an invitation from Her Majesty the Queen, to go to Buckingham Palace to actually meet the Queen where she complimented him on his poems and his fundraising efforts. Darryl also won first prize in a world-wide Elvis Presley poem competition which was organised by Graceland - Darryl was invited to Graceland where he performed his prize-winning poems featuring Elvis Presley. Darryl is also due to appear on Britain's Got Talent this year as a stand up comedian and a comedy poet.

This is Darryl's second book of poems - which includes a vast selection of his own poems. From political satire, comedy, spiritual, gospel, romance and all other kinds of poems. There's even a grand selection of comedy scripts featuring Abbott and Costello, Fawlty Towers...The Return! There really is something for everyone in this fascinating book of poems. It is a must-have book for anyone who loves poetry. Please be warned: Once you pick this book up and start to read it - you won't want to put it down again!!!!

There now follows a selection of poems all featuring the meerkat characters – Aleksandr Orlov, Sergei and Oleg. Be truly amazed at their adventures in poem mode all courtesy of Blackpool poet; Darryl Ashton. Enjoy. SIMPLES!!!!

ALEKSANDR ORLOV AND SERGEI PLAY MEERKAT FOOTBALL/SOCCER

My name is Aleksandr
Orlov, and I am now
a meerkat footballer,
I cannot play in the
goal - because I need
to be taller!
I will be the referee,
and Sergei will be in
goal -
Oleg will be meerkat
striker - but he cannot
get the ball?

We are playing in the
England - in the English
Premier League -

Where all the footballers

are very rich - I have

to join indeed.

Playing also in the USA -

and scoring lots of goals,

Sergei is no good - he

always has to crawls!!!!

But, we are the meerkat

professionals - and we

have to play the same,

But if I do not score any

goal - Sergei I will blame.

Off we run onto the pitch -

it is so real grass,

But Sergei looks so daft

in shorts - he's such a

silly ass!!!!

We like the O-Posts -

super blog - they like our

writing friend,

Hello to Sir Darryl Ashton -

he writes a brand new

trend.

We love to play in America -

we feel like movie stars,

But Sergei tries to kiss me -

when I'm watching the

Star Wars!!!!

We also play the soccer - in

sunny Africa -

I run all over the hot land -

we need to drink more

water.

The Meerkat's will play

England - for a silver solid

cup,

But Oleg cannot play today -

he is just a pup!!

Sergei thinks he's the best -

I let him down gently -

He's too old, and far too

slow - he used to run so

speedy!

We have to get real - and

we cannot play the soccer -

We leave that to the humans -

then I give them all a lecture.

Sergei likes the football - and

he plays with his furry pimple -

Now he watches on meerkat

TV - it's all incredibly SIMPLE!!!!

We have to be professional -

and not to be the groovy's,

Being in the English Football
Premier League - is better
than Hollywood Movies.

We do not like to kiss each
other - we shake our claws
to celebrate -
It just doesn't look right -
Sergei knows his fate!!!!
We will always be the better
team - but Sergei is now a
slob;
'Being in charge of IT - and
playing his computermabob!!!!'
So, now we watch the football,
on large screen television -
Welcome to meerkat football -
now it's intermission!!!!!!

BY DARRYL ASHTON

ALEKSANDR ORLOV...FOUNDER OF MEERKAT EMPIRE

My name is Aleksandr Orlov,
founder of Meerkat.com,
And after a hard day's work –
it's good to come home.

My life is good as good – in
my Meerkat big mansion –
But I do have an assistant –
he's old and he never listen!

We are always very busy –
as computermables we
play,
But it is good to sit
comfortables, and have a
lazy day!

Meerkat manor is such a large
house – it is also very nice,
And every night I take a
splash – maybe once or
twice!

I am lord of meerkat manor
it does sound very posh,
But every other weekend –
we like to play the squash!

I am the master – and I work
hard every day –
But recently I take on helper –
his name is servant' Sergei.

We have returned from Africa –
and we saw our little cousins,
It was also very hot, I tell you –

I nearly lost my marbles!

Sergei is a good servant – he
really is so old,
But he plays computermables –
he just won't be told!

We do have many hardships –
it really is no joke,
Once Sergei tried to swallow
a grub – oh he nearly choke!

Whatever happen we are as
one – I even had to beg –
But then we took in little baby
meerkat - her name is Baby
Oleg.

Sergei does change nappy – he

loses lots of sleep -

Sergei also feeds Oleg – oh it

does so make me weep!

Oleg is so challenging – but I

sit and look,

While Sergei feels so down –

he also has to cook!

So now we plan a holiday –

to a seaside town so cool –

We are going the beach –

and the sea, in good old

little' Blackpool.

While Sergei rides the

donkey's – and Oleg chases

seagulls,

I shall prim my fur – it's so

Incredibly simples!

We like the very high tower –
Sergei is scared of heights;
'But Baby Oleg is laughing –
laughs at Sergei's tights!'

I myself, stay in the
ballroom – and claw around
the dance floor,
And when I do the Meerkat
Bop – everyone shouts...
MORE!

Then I see Sergei – and he
comes to have a dance,
While Baby Oleg takes the
floor – she has to seize her
chance!

Soon they are together –

and it is a pretty sight,

But just when the music

stops – and there is an

awful fight.

We then decide to go home –

back to our luxury hotel,

But why is Sergei wetting his

fur – with sticky smelly gel?

We stay in posh hotel suite –

and order lots of grubs,

Because we Meerkats aren't

allowed – to go in any pubs!

Oleg is wearing a cute little

hat – and eating her favourite

jelly,

But Sergei has gained some weight – he now has the skittle belly!

We all decide to hit the pleasure beach – and to go on the scary rides,
But we cannot get anywhere near, as the sea is now high tides!

So we take a lovely new tram ride, and take a tour of the illuminations –
There are lots of people all smiling – doing their celebrations!

We are now all back home and back to work computermables,

And if people ask us if we enjoyed

our holiday; 'it was so incredibly

simples!!!!'

BY DARRYL ASHTON

ALEKSANDR ORLOV AND SERGEI...
JOIN THE EXPENDABLES

My name is Aleksandr Orlov,

and I'm going to,

Together with servant, Sergei,

we'll cause mass hysteria!

We'll join forces with the

Expendables - and team up

with that Rambo' bloke,

We all dress like soldiers -

and this is no joke.

I will have my meerkat

rifle - and missile rockets

too,

But I have to look out for

Sergei - or send him to

the zoo!

He can work the meerkat

telephone - and also the

meerkat radio -

And when we get to the

airport - we all say;

'here we go!!!!'

We will kick the bottoms

of those evil I.S.I.S cretins,

I know Sergei isn't frightened,

but why is he wearing

leggings?

The Expendables we are -

and we aim to destroy the

enemy,

But Sergei keep on moaning -

his stomach is always empty!!!!

But the puppets in the UK

government - they want our

help today,

We must fight these terrorists -

they cause such mass dismay.

Sergei has his computermabob,

and he types like he's so crazy,

We kill all the I.S.I.S scumbags -

and we tuck into mongoose

meat and gravy!!!!

But, Sergei acts like Rambo -

and he really hurt his leg,

But then he thinks of Africa -

and little baby Oleg.

We are now are being so

professional - and Sergei

plays with his furry pimple;

'How did Aleksandr and Sergei

both defeat the terrorists? -

they said it was so...SIMPLE!!!!'

BY DARRYL ASHTON

ALEKSANDR ORLOV MEERKAT MP

My name is Aleksandr Orlov,

and I'm running to be an MP.

It really does sound quite

incredibles, as everything is

free.

But I live in very posh mansion –

and have got lots of money,

I even prim my lovely fur – in

my luxury new study.

I watch the MPs on the Meerkat

TV, and I have to honestly say;

'They all do seem corruptive –

which they think is okay!'

Let me tell you where I'm comings

from – I have to get things right,

But sometimes it can be noisy

here – and I lack sleep every night.

I always am sitting comfortables –

and take soothing bubble bath,

In my mansion just like MPs – I

cannot get the staff.

I do have a little helper – and he

is now quite old

His name is Sergei, but he does

not like to be told!

Sergei is the boss – of the meerkat

IT department –

But sometimes I need to feel his

fur – it causes argument!

But Sergei had a breakdown –

he say I work him hard –

But that didn't wash my fur –

so I called for Scotland Yard!

We do make many plans – for

me to be MP –

But when I wear my gown – I

cannot find my key!

But recently we had delivery –

upon our doorstep cold,

It was baby meerkat – this is

what I'm told!

I want to be an MP – and have

my title tree –

Then I claim more mongoose

meat – as it will be free!

But life is so tough – I cannot

tell you why –

But Sergei cares for baby Oleg –

especially when she cry!

But life is so incredibles – and

I just cannot see,

'That life really would be grand -

as Aleksandr MP!!!!'

ALEKSANDR ORLOV MEETS NIGEL FARAGE

My name is Aleksandr Orlov,

founder of Meerkat empire,

I love to be a UK MP – and

get everything I desire!

I have a very good assistant –

he is honest and polite,

He plays with my

computermabob, all day and

all night.

My good furry friend is Sergei,

he's always pruning his fur,

He is head of my IT – my tea is

loves to stir!

Are you sitting comfortables –

then I will now begin,

I want to be a meerkat MP –

and help myself to sin!

I would claim many expenses –

to blend in with the crew,

But if I get caught fiddling –

I will always blame you!

Meerkat MP – my name will

be in lights,

Fiddling all my expenses –

oh I can see the delights!

I have to be corruptive, and

make Sergei my PA –

But he might have another

breakdown – so I will dock

his pay!

He works so hard you see,

typing all too slow;

'So I have to pull his fur –

he always feels low!'

But I have watched on

Meerkat TV – the Ukip

political party,

I like their immigration

policies – very

wholeheartedly!

But what will he do for

me, and my meerkat

friends?

Will he ban the Mongoose?

so we can all start new

trends?

I will ask Nigel Farage round –

and he can see my big

mansion –

But I will not pay big

mansion tax – I will make

a suggestion!

When Ukip are in power –

and I become his aide,

Maybe he will join me –

in a glass of lucozade?

Now Ukip are a party, to

govern the UK –

Then me and my friend,

Sergei, will shout; 'hip-pip,

hooray!'

We have to be professional –

like Mr Nigel Farage,

And when the general

election comes round – all

we do is charge!

My meerkat empire – compare

.com, will be in Downing

Street,

And me and Nigel Farage –

will dance the meerkat beat!

So as we all sit comfortables,

and play the computermabob,

I drink a meerkat toast to you

now; 'and eat my corn on the

cob!'

Please, do vote for Nigel Farage,

and me, and Sergei too –

And if we all win power – we

will look after you!

You don't want Cameron, Ed,

or Clegg – they are all criminals –

Just vote for Nigel Farage, my

friends – and that is so SIMPLES!!!!

BY DARRYL ASHTON

ALEKSANDR ORLOV AND SERGEI GO TO WIMBLEDON

"Come along Sergei, sit
down and watch the
tennis,
Please do stop messing
around - and being such
a menace?

"We've come to watch
the tennis - at Wimbledon,
so nice,
But Sergei's always
moaning - he wants a
cold choc ice?

"I wish he'd be more
professional - but he

always prunes his fur,
But we come to watch
the tennis - he simply
does not care!!

"He even bring his
computermabob - to
play on internet,
But a furry little tennis
ball came flying over
the net!!

"I was sat all comfortables -
acting professional -
I thought comings to the
Wimbledon - would be oh
so very simple!!!!

"Sergei now wants to play

tennis - but I told him it
is just a racket,
But, he never listens to
me - and the ball, he wants
to whack it!!!!

"Come along Sergei - we
now are going home,
If you can't sit down and
behave yourself, computer
you will roam?

"So off they trotted out of
Wimbledon - but Sergei's
found a pimple,
How did you like the tennis,
Sergei? oh, it was so very
SIMPLE!!!!"

BY Darryl Ashton

THE MEERKAT SUPER FURRY JET...
DESTINATION AFRICA.

The super jet is waiting -

on the runway for take

off,

It is a super furry jet -

but who owns this jet -

a toff?

The name is Aleksandr

Orlov - and co-pilot

Sergei, too,

They are going back

to Africa - on a mission

for me and you.

Aleksandr ties his tie -

and acts so professional -

But just before take off -

Sergei feels ill!

'I don't feel very well,

Sergei tells Aleksandr,

Come, come, now, it

must have been that

dinner!'

Sergei gets out his

crisps - and starts

munching in full flight;

'Aleksandr has had

enough - and causes

quite a fight!'

The computermabob

is working - and Sergei's

fur stands on end,

Aleksandr looks at him -
he's going round the
bend!

Suddenly, they see
Africa - the sun is
shining hot,
Sergei's busy pruning
his fur - and he's found
another spot!

Aleksandr says; 'it is a
little pimple - and it's
on your furry leg,
Then, just by magic -
they see Baby Oleg!
Professionally they
land the plane - and
their smile is as wide

as wide,

But why does baby

Oleg - suddenly go

and hide?

She has to be brought

home - the animal

rights have ordered,

But both Sergei and

Aleksandr - hide in a

small cupboard!

Now they are all on

board - a super furry

jet,

Aleksandr says to Sergei:

"I told you not to fret!"

Now they are back home -

and Oleg's on his feet,

Sergei asks Aleksandr:

"where's our mongoose

meat?"

All are sat around a table

and Sergei starts to play

with his pimple;

'When Oleg asks papa

Aleksandr how he found

him - he says; 'it was oh

so very SIMPLE!!!!'

BY DARRYL ASHTON

MY NAME IS BABY OLEG

My name is Baby Oleg,

and I'm in Africa,

I really miss my papa -

his name is Aleksandr.

I have an uncle called

Sergei, but he has been

acting strange,

He has also turned all

gay - in my eyes this

makes a change!!

Although I'm in Africa -

I miss my uncle Sergei -

He is always busy typing -

in his laboratory!

Sergei is in charge - of

the meerkat IT office,

But papa Aleksandr - he

is always eating toffees.

They have gone to America,

to be in meerkat movies,

But Sergei is acting all so

funny - he hangs out with

the smoothies!!!!

I do fear for Sergei - as

he isn't very well,

He never used to be so

gay - he even prunes his

fur with smelly gel!!!!

I know my papa Aleksandr -

he is so very sad,

He wants the old Sergei to

come back - and he is so

hopping mad!!

I can only pray in Africa -

for uncle Sergei now,

I pray he gets better - and

free from his sin, somehow!!

But, now, I stay in Africa -

as I don't like America -

They stab their food and

pick it up - without any care!!

I do love England more -

and papa Aleksandr's big

mansion,

And if Sergei doesn't turn

straight again - it really

will be treason.

Why is life so difficult - it

should be very simple,

But Sergei plays all the

time - with his furry pimple.

I love uncle Sergei a lot -

and I know he hears my

call;

'But, the next time I see

uncle Sergei - he must

act professional!!!!'

My name is Baby Oleg - and

now I say; 'goodbye',

I cry all the way to Africa -

as Sergei is a spy!

Papa Aleksandr, is nowhere

to be seen,

He is so upset - he says;

'Sergei is a QUEEN!!!!'

I will now go to America -

and campaign like never

before,

And when I see the gay

rights people - I'll quickly

close the door!!!!

God bless you all - and

Sergei too - he is a queen

to beg;

'Goodbye my friends - I wish

you well - from a happy

Baby Oleg.'

Compare the market is now

running smoothies,

And we would like to

welcome you all - to the

Meerkat Hollywood Movies!!!!

BY DARRYL ASHTON

THE RESCUE OF BABY OLEG

What is happening in

Africa? - and to the TV

meerkats?

They've dumped baby

Oleg there - oh, the

little prats!!

Why have they left

him in the heat - in

sunny Africa?

You must bring him

home straight away -

he may catch the

Ebola!!

Aleksandr Orlov, you

should feel well

ashamed -

Dumping Baby Oleg -
is Sergei going to be
blamed?
You play on your
computermabob - all
day, and all night,
But you have to go
and get Oleg - leaving
him in Africa - it just
isn't right!!

Someone may call,
the animal rights
protection police;
'And if this gets out
on national TV -
they'll feel your
furry fleece!!'
Will Sergei have a

breakdown? Or,

will you do the right

thing?

And go and get baby

Oleg - and then you

can start to sing!

It really is incredibles -

what you both have

done,

You have to return to

Africa - and bring baby

Oleg back home.

You can both fly by jet -

in first class meerkat

plane,

Or Sergei and the

nation - will all go

insane!!

While Aleksandr Orlov

sits in his pilot seat,

Co-Pilot, Sergei - checks

his meerkat fleet!

So, while Sergei plays

with his computermabob -

and his new found pimple;

As you both fly to Africa -

it really is so SIMPLE!!!!

Now they have come

home - they've all been

professional -

And even baby Oleg -

he's dancing on the

table!!

Life is good as good -

in our own big mansion

home,

But sometime next year,

again, off to Africa - we

all shall freely roam!!

BY DARRYL ASHTON

SAVE OUR SERGEI...SET SERGEI FREE.

I am Aleksandr Orlov, and

I'm feeling very sad,

Sergei doesn't want

anymore - and now I'm

hopping mad!

He loves Nicole Kidman -

and he wants to be a

man,

He doesn't like being

gay - or classed as a

tran!!!!

He is what he is - but

he is always moaning

about,

How can he be normal

meerkat - his gender's

up the spout!!!!

He has to face this

problem - and accept

that he is gay,

But in PC Britain - being

gay is okay!!!!

He is a furry gray hatter,

and he's now so depressed,

He knows that he is gay -

and he feels so second

best.

I tell him to accept it -

but that just makes him

mad,

He knows that being gay -

will always be classed as

bad.

Sergei is trying everything,

to be a normal meerkat,

But, I tell him he is gay -

there's no doubt about

that!!!!

Nicole Kidman just feels

sorry - as she thinks old

Sergei's cute,

She has got her suspicions,

that Sergei is a fruit!!!!

I tell Sergei to; 'get a grip' -

no, not of my furry widget!

He tries so hard to ignore

the fact - so he plays with

his furry giblet!!!!

He has to carry on - and

live his life with me,

And when we're back at

home - he can sit upon my

knee!!!!

Sergei is still my friend -

and he always makes my

tea.

He is also very reliable - he's

head of meerkat IT!!!!

He now works so hard for

me - I treat him like a slave,

Well, all he does is cry a lot -

I wish he would behave?

He plays with his computermabob,

he treats everything as

essential.

He knows he is getting old -

so he tries to be professional!!!!

I tell him; 'being gay is acceptable,

but he still plays with his furry pimple.'

Maybe one day he'll feel better, and stop acting so...SIMPLE!!!!!!

But I now have bought him some medicine, that will do the trick.

He now shall be a normal Sergei - and now he may just click!!!!

I will be very patient with Sergei - but he cannot be a man:

'No matter what he does - just ask Nicole Kidman!!!!'

Sergei is very depressed - and has lost the will to live.

But he must accept he isn't straight - his gender, he should forgive!
He is the only Sergei - the only gay in the village,
But his tormented soul is now fed up - he wants to go to the vicarage!

Back at the restaurant, Sergei eats his mongoose mince,
But, why is Aleksandr grinning - and his lips start to wince!
Aleksandr tells Sergei; 'is the mongoose mince good - you eat it for your supper?'
But, if you eat too much of mince - it'll turn you into a meerkat puffta!!!!

The moral of this story - and

for the sake of poor Sergei,

Being gay is now okay - but

Sergei still feels such dismay.

But who has heard of a

meerkat - being married to

his IT,

But if this makes Sergei happy -

and it sets his gender FREE!!!!

NICOLE KIDMAN HAS BEEN DUMPED

Nicole Kidman is down in

the dumps,

As Sergei chooses and

picks his new chumps.

Nicole sits and looks so

depressed -

As Aleksandr is Sergei's

new special guest.

Nicole can't believe she's

not going to the movies,

She has been dumped

by a couple of smoothies.

Nicole Kidman puts on her

new hat,

She feels so humiliated

by a gay meerkat!

Sergei has choses his new cinema date,
Will this decision now seal Sergei's fate?
Sat in the cinema eating popcorn - and having fun,
While poor Nicole has now become a nun!

A simples date which Nicole enjoyed -
But now she's been dumped - she's so very annoyed.
She wished she'd brought her new mobile camera.
To film the jealous - the

gay Aleksandr!!!!

Nicole is playing with

her computermabob,

But Sergei is playing with

furry little knob!!!!

Aleksandr and Sergei

sit and hold claws,

Why did Sergei choose

Aleksandr? God only

knows!!!!

So, there you have it -

the truth is out,

Nicole Kidman is now

up the spout!!!!

she isn't pleased - and

her tummy looks fat;

'That's what you get -

from a "GAY" meerkat!!!!'

From a life of simples -

and Hollywood Movies,

Aleksandr and Sergei

are a couple of smoothies.

They play together with

each other's furry pimple,

And together they act so

incredibly...SIMPLE!!!!!!

SERGEI'S HOT DATE AT THE RESTAURANT - FEATURING NICOLE KIDMAN – FEATURING A VERY JEALOUS ALEKSANDR ORLOV

I am Aleksandr Orlov,

and I'm not very happy,

Sergei is on a hot date -

and he's also very chatty!

He's gone to a very posh

restaurant - and he's

acting like a human,

And I'm very upset - he's

dating Nicole Kidman!

I will have to gatecrash,

and make my feelings

known,

I can't have Sergei turning

normal - he's venturing

into the unknown!

But I have set up meerkat

spy camera - and I'm

watching his furry maggot,

But I can't have Sergei

turning into - a slippery

meerkat faggot!!!!

I pop up at the restaurant,

where Nicole and Sergei

are sat,

Who is Sergei trying to

kid? Will I doff my hat?

I have to give him an

option - make him choose

his date;

'But, if he chooses Nicole

Kidman - I make sure he

knows his fate!'

Nicole is after Sergei's

computermabob, which

Sergei always plays on,

But who will Sergei choose

to be with? That is the

burning question!

Sergei sits at the table - he

doesn't know what to do -

He seems to relish the fact -

but he acts like he's in a

zoo!

I'll have a prawn cocktail -

and that is just a start,

If I have the rollmop

herring - it might just make

me fart!!!!

Sergei is drinking wine -

and being rather silly,

But why does he wear a

posh napkin - I think he's

turning screwy!!!!

Then we have the main

course - some very tasty

mongoose steak,

But giving Sergei a finger

bowl - was a big mistake.

Now Sergei has the skittle

belly - and he's on a very

hot date.

Will Nicole Kidman pinch

his furry face - or will

Aleksandr win his mate?

Sergei plucks up the courage

to play a crafty trick,

He won't allow Aleksandr to

touch his spotted dick!!!!

Sergei sits and prunes his

fur - and Aleksandr is upset.

Nicole Kidman tells Sergei:

"You are my furry pet!!"

They now have reached a

crisis - over who will pay the

food bill,

While Nicole Kidman goes

to the loo - she's gone to take

a pill!

While Nicole Kidman pleads

with Sergei: "Please come

home with me?"

Sergei says: "I'm so confused

and I need a wee!"

So, who will win Sergei's

heart, - and enjoy a new hot

date?

Please do vote on the meerkat

phone - before it is too late!

So Aleksandr makes eyes

at Nicole Kidman - and he

try's to be professional;

'Glaring as he says to Sergei;

'what you are doing is so

very criminal!!!!'

So, Nicole Kidman walks

away in tears - as Sergei

chooses his mate.

I think Nicole was lovely -

nice than Aleksandr, his

jealous' new date!!!!

Sitting at the table, and

pruning each other's

furry pimple,

Sergei tried to go straight -

but it wasn't all that simple!

But now they leave the restaurant and they both do feel a thrill;
'Walking "claw in claw" - not acting so professional!!!!'
Will Sergei get another chance - as Aleksandr will make him choose,
Or will poor little Sergei not see sense - and act like a sorry little "son-of-a-mongoose!!!!"

BONFIRE NIGHT WITH ALEKSANDR ORLOV

My name is Aleksandr Orlov,

founder of meerkat empire,

And every bonfire night – we

always light big fire.

Now I don't like the fireworks,

they're too loud for baby Oleg,

But all the family meerkats –

come to visit, and beg!

I have to watch Sergei, he loves

his meerkat friends,

But he always plays with the

fireworks – driving me round

the bend.

I have to be professional – as

Sergei tends the fire,

Lifting all the wood – I say;

'Sergei, lift it higher?'

It looks so incredibles – the
noise is really deafening,
Now I hear Sergei – but why
is he singing?
The bonfire is a-light – and
Oleg is enthralled,
But Sergei is complaining –
he says he is cold!

Sparklers are everywhere,
and hot mongoose soup is
being served,
The sight is so incredibles,
just what we all deserved.
The fire is burning brightly,
and Sergei is now all warm,
But baby Oleg is hungry –

and she's cooking up a

storm!

I will now stand back from

the fire, I don't want to singe

my fur,

While Sergei tends to the

meerkat broth — by giving

it a stir.

Sergei is now getting quite

carried away — and starts to

shout...OLAY!!

Why won't he listen to me —

I feel in meerkat dismay?

I have thrown big bonfire

party-fire, at my big posh

mansion,

But sadly some could not

make it – especially Papa
Anton.
I have to now call time –
on my luxury meerkat
bonfire,
But don't forget to buy
your meerkat toy, before
they all catch fire!
Happy Bonfire Night I
say to you – and I mean
that most sincerely;
'Enjoy the bonfire night
celebrations – as Oleg
looks a cutie!'
Another bonfire is all
finished – and Sergei
plays with his furry
pimple –
Ask him if he enjoyed

the meerkat fireworks –

he'll say incredibly...

SIMPLE!!!!

POOR SERGEI

My name is Aleksandr Orlov,

and I have a little problem,

Sergei has turned all gay –

and he tries to touch my

furry bottom.

We went to Blackpool town

and saw some people

marching,

They all looked so peculiar –

and I wasn't really laughing!

I am very disappointed how

Blackpool has now changed,

It used to attract nice families –

now it attracts the deranged!

I feel so sorry for Sergei – but

he might soon get better,

And be his normal self again —

instead of a mad-hatter!!

He used to play on his

computermabob — all day and

all night,

But now he acts so girly — he

gives me such a fright!!

I will not allow this — as I want

the old Sergei back —

But if he stays a little gay — he

will soon get the sack!

I cannot leave him with Oleg

as I couldn't trust his way,

I just cannot understand —

why he has turned so gay????

I really do blame Blackpool —

for it really does attract,

The wrong kind of people –

or is it just an act?

My relatives in Meerkovo –

are all saddened by this news,

They just cannot believe it –

and they definitely are not

amused!!

I know Sergei has been

working hard – and he has not

been well,

But he cannot be different –

he'll end up in a prison cell!

We do not have little gay

meerkats – that is for the

humans –

I will not tolerate this camp

behaviour – he has to be

normals!!!!

I'll send him back to Africa –

to his cousins there,

But I warn Sergei for his best –

they won't like him, I swear!

They might put him on a

fire – and roast his furry nuts,

And then all go drinking – in

their little meerkat huts!

Sergei will not be popular –

he'll have to change his ways,

They will not accept a meerkat

being gay – it may be just a

phase!!

I have to get him some help –

the meerkat doctor will know,

Then, when Sergei is normal

again – we'll put him on show!

You, see, all I want is normality,

not Sergei' a little camp -

All this news about Sergei – it

really gives me the cramp!!

But we do have to be

professional – and help Sergei

to get better,

Not leave him as he is – a

meerkat...furry mad-hatter!!!!

I see him every day - playing

with his furry pimple –

And someone told me – that

Sergei's gone all SIMPLE!!!!

BY DARRYL ASHTON

There now follows a poem featuring the magical concert of Shakin' Stevens.

THE MAGICAL CONCERT OF SHAKIN' STEVENS

He sang about a Green Door,

and about This Ole House,

Oh Julie was so Satisfied,

that she scared a little mouse!

Turning Away the mouse

sure did - and running into

the Raindrops,

While Shaky sang; 'Give Me

Your Heart Tonight' - on

good old Top Of The Pops.

Shaky had a Love Attack, and

his woman cried; I Might,

While Shaky said; 'You Shake

Me Up' - they'll Tear It Up

tonight.

Shaky did his concert - and

sang; My Cutie Cutie,

He also drank some Pink

Champagne - turning very fruity!

Shaky did the Queen of The

Hop - as he was Rockin' The

Night Away,

He pounced into Shake Rattle

And Roll - and sang it with

Jealousy.

Shaky grabbed the microphone -

and sang about 'Hot Dog' for me,

He sang about Josephine, but

he was loving Marie Marie!

Shaky was in Trouble, and he had a Love Attack!
Then he sang True Love to an adoring fan, but she gave him such a whack!
Shaky was singing Elvis - as he curled his Lipstick, Powder & Paint -
But singing Merry Christmas Everyone - he really felt quite faint.

Shaky was so Lovestruck, and also Without Love,
He even sang of a Shotgun Boogie, but he couldn't get enough!

Shaky growled through Hey

Mae, because he said; It's Late -

When he drooled on Little

Pigeon - it would seal his

singing fate!

Shaky bopped to Apron

Springs, and pounded to

Shooting Gallery -

He had a love for Vanessa -

and sang his Boppity Bop,

Singing Que Sera, Sera,

he nearly through a strop!

Shaky thought of Mona Lisa -

as he sang his; I'm Knockin'

The stage was his own Sea

Of Love - as he carried on

his boppin!!!!

Shaky growled through; The

Bop Won't Stop - and he

sprang into Diddle I -

He crooned through; A Love

Worth Waiting For,

Then he said goodbye -

as the fans all screamed

for more!!!!

BY DARRYL ASHTON

There now follows a BRILLIANT selection of poems featuring the legendary KING of rock n roll – ELVIS PRESLEY - All written by the stand-up comedian, and comedy poet – Darryl Ashton. Enjoy!

ELVIS PRESLEY SINGS WITH THE ROYAL PHILHARMONIC ORCHESTRA.

The brilliant Royal Philharmonic
Orchestra are really so supreme,
They are teaming up with Elvis
Presley - to sing; 'If I Can Dream.'
Elvis does stand there as the
orchestra begins to play,
And Elvis sings his way through -
the classic; 'My Way'.

The Royal Philharmonic Orchestra
play their instruments loudly,
As Elvis Presley belts out the
classic; 'American Trilogy'.
The whole orchestra follows Elvis
and they wait for their queue,
Then Elvis belts out loud - the

brilliant; 'The Wonder Of You'.
Elvis sings his heart out - that is so evident to see,
While The Royal Philharmonic Orchestra all play with magic glee.
The songs are coming thick and fast - as Elvis wears his bling,
Confirming to the audience - he really is the king.

The orchestra stays with him - and the music does get higher,
And Elvis belts out the classic song: 'See See Rider.'
The audience are in raptures, as the orchestra know their role,
And Elvis does a mean version - of the stunning; 'King Creole.'

The orchestra sounds so
very clever,
As Elvis sings It's Now Or
Never,
The backing singers are
at the alter,
As Elvis serenades with;
'Bridge Over Troubled
Water'.

As Elvis stands there
having a drink of ice tea,
The orchestra play; 'It's
Always Me'.
Elvis smiles and the crowd
shout; 'MORE' -
So Elvis pines through; 'In
The Ghetto'.

This concert is magic - as
God did choose,
And Elvis belts out the:
'Steamroller Blues'.
This CD should be put in
to your checkout cart,
As you listen to Elvis sing;
'How Great Thou Art'.

Elvis bows to the Royal
Philharmonic,
As his voice sounds so
awesome - and pure
magic.
The Royal Philharmonic
Orchestra - has pleased
Elvis Presley,
Computer magic - is Elvis's'
destiny.

This magical concert is a must

for Elvis fans,

And everyone in the audience -

are excitingly clapping their

hands.

The Royal Philharmonic Orchestra

was sent from heaven, above,

While Elvis brings the curtain

down with; 'Can't Help Falling

In Love.'

BY DARRYL ASHTON

THE LEGEND...ELVIS PRESLEY

(I dedicate this poem to all
the true Elvis Presley fans
around the world. God Bless
you Elvis Presley - the KING.)

Waiting in the wings
just to go out and
sing,
I glance on down at
my white shoes - and
all my fancy bling.
Nervous I am - as the
people shout real
loud -
Sounds like a dream
come true - oh what a
crowd?

Suddenly like a king -

I walk sternly onto

the stage -

Unleashing my songs

to the crowd - like an

animal from a cage!

My hair jet black - and

my suit virgin white,

I am so very nervous -

but I will be alright.

I throw my guitar around

my neck to play,

Now I'll let rip - I now feel

okay.

Strumming the guitar is

what I do kike to do -

But singing my songs - is

what I'll do for you.

Shaking my leg - and

singing out loud -

The noise is awesome -

coming from the crowd.

I feel like the king - the

king that I am -

Who would have thought

this - straight from my

pram?

My name is Elvis Presley,

and I will always be here,

Because without a song -

you might just shed a tear.

I watch from the heaven's,

as paradise is my new

home,

But no one can take my

crown away - as I wear it

here - it is known.

I now sing with the angels

as they really are magical -

So from Elvis Presley - I

now bow out - and in heaven,

it is so special.

I'm with my mom and dad,

and also twin brother, Jessie,

We are all so happy now -

at peace, and oh so happy.

God bless the king - king

Elvis Presley,

We will never forget you -

you are the king...OKAY.

You are now a legend - and

you always will be to the

world,

The legend Elvis Presley -

the story will be told.

You were sadly taken from

us - and taken much too

soon,

But when the women saw

you - all they did was swoon!

I end my little tribute - and

now I do salute you,

God bless you, Elvis Presley -

you are the king - to true.

BY DARRYL ASHTON

A KID WITH SIDEBURNS

A kid with sideburns, and

a snarl, sang a song for his

momma today,

The sound was different –

the boy was so shy – but

clutching his guitar – he

began to play.

What's going on, shouted

Sam Philips, in shock?

We don't know, sir, but

this kid really does rock!

Taking a coffee break was

to change the music world,

The boy, Elvis, has to be

told.

From a hillbilly cat – to Elvis

The pelvis,

His appearance did glow –

he knew how to impress.

Wiggling he did – he just had

to move,

Gyrating his hips – he really

felt the groove.

A shy young man – who

played his guitar –

Sam Philips did say; "this kid

will go far!"

From Tupelo to Memphis -

from the movies to Vegas,

The world was meeting Elvis -

he was sheer class.

BY DARRYL ASHTON

ELVIS…(MY VALENTINE)

I was All Shook Up about you,

Love Me Tender from the start,

I'll spend my life just Loving You,

Don't have a Wooden Heart.

It's Now or Never Valentine,

You're my Latest Flame it's true,

Wear my Ring Around Your Neck,

Because I'm really Stuck On You.

I wish that you would Treat Me Nice,

And Surrender to my woo's,

Let's Rock a Hula Baby,

And I'll wear my Blue Suede Shoes.

Be my Teddy Bear and my Good Luck Charm,

And to nobody else Don't Tell,

And if I ever wanted One Night With You,

It would be in Heartbreak Hotel.

I had my Suspicion about you,

You were The Girl of My Best Friend,

I'm so proud you're not in the Ghetto,

And love A fool such as I in the end.

(Have a nice day from Elvis)

ELVIS...THE CONCERT BUILD UP

I waited in the hallway

but I wanted to runaway,

I was nervous – oh so

nervous, I felt my soul

giving way?

I could hear the noise of

the people, they really

were shouting,

I had to go on stage – and

sing like a king?

It really was an occasion,

no other person had

achieved,

But I would go out there –

and simply sing indeed?

The intro started – boy I

was scared, but I had to

go on –

The orchestra was playing

good, I even heard the

drum!

My costume was white, with

gold and blue, it was my turn

to shine,

Being out there in Hawaii, boy,

it felt so fine?

The moment a legend would

really make his mark,

And I was so exited – ready to

recreate that spark!

That spark I had in Hollywood,

it really was a buzz,

But some of those stupid movies,

boy, what a load of fuss?

My time in Hollywood, was

now coming to a close,

I made some awful movies,

but, I made some good ones,

of course?

But back to the present, I was

back, had I been away?

I was ready to sing See See

Rider – and feel my body just

sway!

The occasion would be filmed,

and seen by millions,

But I felt good – and raring to

go, I'm set for battle stations!

I stood there tall – as tall as a

king, my future would secure,

I stormed on out there to the

stage, boy, they wanted more?

Parading proudly across the stage,

it felt so exciting,

The audience in their thousands –

were really so inviting?

I took on hold of my guitar and

swung it round my neck,

I walked up to the microphone,

the feel, I had to check!

Singing loudly as I do, there was

no going back,

The concert was a complete

success, I hadn't lost the knack!

Thank you to Hawaii, and the

audience so true,

My Aloha From Hawaii was —

especially for you!

My nerves had gone, and I

was there, were I did belong,

Up on that great big stage —

singing all my songs?

Just to hear the audience roar,

I really was in awe,

The more I sang — the more the

cries, they really did all roar!

I felt like jelly but so good, the

concert was a success,

I was back where I belonged, I

felt like Elliott Ness!

All my nerves which I had, had

now totally disappeared,

I would now go to all my shows,

never more to be feared.

I have to thank all my friends,

and of course, my band,

They have always been there –

and closely watch my hand?

My orchestra too, they are

supreme, I couldn't ask for

more,

When they played the over-

ture, the audience did roar!

I was now back in Hawaii, and

a concert all so true,

Thank you to all my fans – my

God, I do love all of you.

This would mark my concert

tours, and baby, I am yours,

Thank you to my holy lord,

he really opened my doors?

I was to play Las Vegas, and

tour the United States,

I would never leave any concert,

the lord, he does create?

Ladies and gentlemen, my health

was poor, but I did carry on,

But my singing voice, and my zest,

would always light my throne.

I now sit here in heaven – and look
upon down,
Down on the earth, and to my fans –
please don't wear that frown?

I am at peace and I sing in heaven,
as the lord loves to hear,
I am with my mom, and my dad,
my greatest fans so dear.

Mourn not, for I shall be back,
when the time is right,
For destiny is in the future –
the lord tells it straight?

I did it My Way, and I loved my
life, and the Aloha From Hawaii,
Please say a prayer just for me,
and I'll never leave you, I pray.

The king is in heaven, and does still sing, so salute the name of
Elvis,
For he opened his heart at every concert, and all was sheer bliss!
Aloha From Hawaii is now a legacy, it creates the sound so pure,
Turning the name of Elvis, to a legend, now for sure?

This concert is now available, and Elvis listens on,
He looks at his mom – who looks at the lord, and says: "that's my very proud son?".

THE END

THE BOY...ELVIS!

There was a boy who was born

To parents who's love was known

They knew poverty and hunger

And they wished for things to get better.

This is a poem about such amazing events

And how one child would change the likes

Of music forever and be known as the king

And truly a legacy was would bring

Pleasure to the world and all those who heard

The amazing voice of a child

Who would grow up and change the world

Of music that was so dearly loved.

The boy Elvis, had a gift from God

And he really would change the world.

He would sit on the lap of his mother
And hum to a song like no other.

Yes, Elvis was different, in so many ways
And he seemed to sway to the music with ease.
Only a child but he remarkably had
A gift that would make him glad

The boy Elvis had a twin brother
But he was stillborn when he came from his mother
Elvis would be the only child
But he'd remember his twin as he smiled.

As a child Elvis would dream
About one day he'd learn to hum
And sing the words to a lovely song
Which one day would make him the king

Elvis would soon take to the stage

And belt out the songs with ease.

But his life would be short

and he'd be called by his God

To perform in heaven for the Lord

ELVIS IN CONCERT

Hello Elvis, how are you today?
Oh, I'm okay, I guess – I feel I
need to pray.
Are you worried about tonight -
and the concert hall hotel?
Yes, sir, I am – and the audience,
I really hope we gel.

Elvis goes backstage to put on
his jumpsuit,
The famous white and gold
bold eagle – it really does look
cute.
Standing there like a God, as
only Elvis does,
Elvis shakes and twitches – he
can't believe the fuss.

The theme A Space Odyssey,

starts to fill the arena,

As Elvis stands there just like

a God – looking tanned and

clutching a vodka!

He takes a last sip – and he

walks out on to the stage,

Where he unleashes all his

energy – like an animal in

a cage!

With his guitar wrapped around

him – he walks towards the

microphone,

Taking hold with such vigour – his

voice just belts out; I'm home!"

Bursting into See See Rider, and

hotly into Burning Love,

His amazing voice – he hasn't lost –

which came from God, above.

From You Gave Me A Mountain –

and a cracking Jailhouse Rock,

He almost burst into a version of –

Rock Around The Clock!

Blue Hawaii from paradise, and

always a Good Luck Charm,

He said to a lady; Tickle Me, and

she Gently took his arm.

He had a Suspicious Mind,

but he just drove on a Long

Lonely Highway –

Thinking about; The Girl Of My

Best Friend, he sang the songs

My Way.

He thought he heard a Hound

Dog, and a Shake Rattle and

Roll,

He felt like a King Creole, and

and felt like a Lover Doll.

The audience all loved him –

and five encores soon did

follow a beam,

But he had to close the

show sometime - as he was

to Follow That Dream.

As the sweat poured from his

brow,

He was soon to give his final

bow.

The silence was so eerie – as

he sang; Can't Help Falling In

Love,

And he threw his cape to the

people, as they frantically tried

to shove.

Elvis was clutching a crown –

he stood so dynamic –

The show really was – super

and so magic.

His band played on as Elvis

left the stage – feeling so

relieved,

Elvis had performed like the

King he was – he really was

so afraid!

Thank you God, Elvis said – as

backstage he praised the lord,

For giving him the talents –

which everyone adored.

We thank the lord for giving

us a singer with such emotion,

And in his short lifetime – the

world he showed such devotion.

God bless you, Elvis, as we all

will Remember You,

May the American Trilogy, be

with you – as we all do love

you true.

THE END

ELVIS MEETS HAYLEY DAVIES

As Elvis belts out his songs

to everyone at the front,

His amazing status went

from the stage, to all like

a stunt!

The awesome power of his

voice,

Gave him the gift to sing

any choice.

As he finished his last concert,

which was filmed live from

the turf ,

Elvis said to his friend, I

need to back down to

the earth?

I saw a lady who was waving
at me.
And I thought she was going
down on one knee?

The lady called Hayley Davies,
she just danced away all night,
Oh she really was a beauty, and
a sheer delight.

Hayley danced to Blue Suede
Shoes, as if she felt the beat,
Then smooched along to Love
Me Tender, oh, she looked a
treat.

Then I sang Treat Me Nice, to

which Hayley, who did care,

As her love for me was like

Loving You, Hayley was a star!

The audience was screaming,

to the Jailhouse Rock,

When all of a sudden – Hayley

lost her sock!

With everyone jiving to Hound

Dog, so very loud,

She sang Teddy Bear, Hayley,

to the crowd?

I invited her up on to the stage,

where we both sang a duet,

I looked Hayley in to her eyes,

Gently, I'll never forget.

I couldn't help thinking - that's

The Wonder of You,

Oh, to my special friend, Hayley,

i'll always be Almost Always True!

We could be in Blue Hawaii, and

dance to Slicin' Sand,

While you Kiss Me Quick, as we

walk hand in hand.

My time down on the earth, now,

It's Over,

I have to take the Long Lonely

Highway, as the Moody Blue is

appearing?

I Gently kissed Hayley, and boy,

the earth did move.

I had the American Trilogy feeling,

that, Tonight Is So Right For Love!

I've enjoyed meeting Hayley Davies,

who's been my Good Luck Charm,

I'll never ever forget you Hayley, I

love you like my mom.

The concert had finished,

the lights did so flash,

And Hayley to the stage,

she did so dash!

Hayley had met the man

of her dreams,

King Elvis, you still reign

so supreme.

Back in the space ship Elvis

did go,

As he waved goodbye to

Hayley,

he whispered, And I love

You So.

Beyond The Bend he flew,

back to, This Is My Heaven,

Goodbye, Elvis, Forever True,

You'll Never Walk Alone.

Hayley, you'll always be, The

Girl of My Best Friend,

And I just, Can't Help Falling

In Love, with you till the very

end.

We'll never have Suspicion, as

we don't have a Wooden Heart,

But meeting Hayley Davies, is

a love to never part.

God Bless you, Elvis, we made

a fantastic team,

I guess us meeting again, I really

can...If I Can Dream.

BY DARRYL ASHTON

ELVIS THE PELVIS

I walk on to the stage –

so nervous as heck –

Is this my future – I am

to trek?

My soul feels the music –

that I do know,

But sometimes I do feel

so terribly low.

Of course, I get nervous –

before each show –

My heart is pumping –

this I know.

When I'm on stage – I do

let loose –

Sometimes I drink some

good old fruit juice.

The hillbilly cat, is what

they call me –

And; Elvis the pelvis – it

was given for free.

I do feel the music – that

is for sure,

I sing and gyrate – that is

the cure.

People screaming – bedlam

is here,

My mama is worried – don't

worry my dear.

I move to the music – it's just

what I do,

All this and more – I do for

you.

My legs are shaking with a
mind of their own –
Now I am sat upon my thrown.
They call me the king of rock
and roll,
Boy, oh boy, I feel ten foot
tall!

My name is Elvis Presley, and
I am real shy,
This is so true – I cannot deny.
But my music helps me to
express myself,
As my life is much busier – I
amass great wealth.

Records are made – and a
home I buy,
The beautiful Graceland – for

my mommas to try.

All the good things I give to

my mom,

And she pats me gently upon

my tum!

My momma is my rock – my

guardian angel,

But now she's gone – I am

not able.

My life means nothing – but

the show must go on,

I have no one else to turn too,

I want to just run.

The good lord says; "go, and

entertain the excited crowds –

Use that voice – and you'll

have no doubts?"

The hillbilly cat is here to stay,

As I get ready – I need to pray.

The rest is history – and is a

legend –

When the final curtain bowed,

his soul did amend.

The pelvis is the king – and he

always will be,

Elvis the pelvis – the true king

you see.

BY DARRYL ASHTON

(There now follows a selection of poems with the subject of (MY NAME IS:). A mixture of comedy, religious and political satire. Enjoy!)

MY NAME IS ALFRED GARNETT

(With apologies to Johnny Speight)

My name is Alfred Garnett,

and I'm married to a silly

moo,

'Every time I come home

from work - she tells me

what to do!'

I am a Tory supporter -

well, someone has to be -

I keep on praising Ted

Heath - he lived at bleak

house for free!

I work very hard every

day - and I have a little

groan,

And when I was told to

work a three day week -

oh, I really did have a

moan!

I like to smoke my pipe

a lot - but the tobacco

costs too much -

It is my only pleasure -

the sex is out of touch!!

We now have a new

home help - his name

is Marigold Winston -

But because he's like

a woman - I call it

bloody treason!

He prances about in a

pinny - and he talks

in an African dialect -

Why did the bloody

council pick him? Could

they not be a bit more

select?

Now I call him Marigold -

he's always prancing

about,

He really is an eyesore -

he always has to shout!

But he does know his

place - he loves his

kitchen duties,

He cooks and cleans

like a demented queen -

and he cleans my dirty

britches!

My wife, Else, God Bless

her soul - is up in

heaven now,

But the DHSS stopped

her pension - she's left

me skint - the cow!

I've called the social

services - they are no

bloody good,

They act just like the

DHSS - they don't pay

me like they should!

My name is Alfred

Garnett - and I often

have a beer -

It is my only pleasure -
now I've lost my, Elsie'
dear!

People say I'm a racist -
and a bigot, and a
whinger,
I think they've got the
wrong person - some
said I was their saviour!!!!

I love to watch West Ham -
(up the hammers) - and
watch it all for nothing;
'I even used a wheelchair -
while the stewards weren't
looking!!'

I want to say goodbye

to you - and I thank you

for being true,

Oh, how I miss my Elsie -

that bloody silly moo!!

BY DARRYL ASHTON

MY NAME IS ALI BABA

My name is Ali Baba,

and I have got forty

thieves,

We steal lots of

treasure, and shove

it up our sleeves.

I know a bloke called

Salmond, he talks a

load of nonsence,

But all he really wants;

is Scottish independence!

My name is Ali Baba –

and my friends love the

UK –

We take advantage of

your benefits – then we

all do pray!

We claim asylum as we
come here – and we like
a drink of beer,
But all we really want to
do – is cause a lot of fear.

My name is Ali Baba –
and we love the British
folk,
But all we really want to
do – is hope they all do
choke!
I have a motley crew –
and Britain is our aim,
To cause you all mass
terror – it really is a
game!

The European rights – is
what we all adore,
We are all taken care of –
when we come through
your door?
If we are refused entry –
then all we do is claim;
"Our human rights to your
benefits – it really is a
game!"

My religion is a secret –
but being Christian is
not for us,
Islam is what we love –
we will cause such a
fuss!
We are all part of a
group – of scallywags,

that's for sure,
We've taken over many
shops now – your money
we adore!

My name is Ali Baba, my
friend is Greedy Sinbad –
We talk in our own tongue,
we really are so bad.
We do employ a lot of staff,
but they must be chocolate
brown,
And when the immigration
call – we do put on a frown!

We like the United Kingdom,
well, we get a grant for free.
To start up a newsagents –
and high prices are the key!

We all have mobile phones —

all are state-of-the-art,

And when we've eaten all our

curry — we let off a smelly

fart!

We do have to tolerate, the

English who come in —

But when they give us their

hard earned money — they

think it is a sin!

We rub our hands with olive

oil, then Popeye comes

along,

Helping cousin, Bluto — to

come to evensong!

The council too are good to

us — and at no extra cost —

They also have all built for
us - a brand new cosy mosque!
We pray to Allah – he's our
saviour – and also our boss –
But when we hear about
Christianity – we really don't
give a toss!

When Christmas comes we
do care – but, not about baby
Jesus,
But opening up our expensive
shop – and making no such
fuss!
All we want is money – and to
heck with Christianity –
Then we're all together – those
Christians, we do all pity.

My name is Ali Baba – I come

from Bongo Bongo –

But every year I take a tour,

of the sweaty Congo Congo!

I do have many family – that

is very true,

Britain is our destiny – new

wealth for my thieving crew!

I love my Captain Sinbad – he

tried to kiss me once –

I said; back off matey – and

called him a thieving nonce!

I am now happily married –

with ten wives to support,

So now I'm in the UK – I can

claim Income Support!

My name is Ali Baba – and

this is my own story,

But now I am hungry – I need

to eat my curry!

From Bongo Bongo land – oh

so far away –

I'm happy now in the UK – my

benefit's they will pay!

My name is Ali Baba – and

I'm going to the U.S.A, -

Where Obama will join us in

our den – and then we all

shall pray.

But they don't pay us any

welfare – we haven't paid

any insurance,

So they deport us back to

Britain – where we are a

bloody nuisance!

My name is Ali Baba – and
now I'm home in the UK –
A land of milk and honey –
and we will be okay!
I have many friends in
France – but they all live in
tents,
They want to cross the
channel – they all are
relative immigrants!

We are now all settled, in
the UK, for eternity,
That is now the case – now
where's my bleeding money?!
The paleface will be the
minority – and Sharia Law
shall rule,
Please don't underestimate

us all – we're nobody's fool!

My name is Ali Baba – I own

a kebab shop –

But where's all that treasure

gone – someone call a cop?

We are all very happy – as we

are all staying – Enoch Powell

was a fright;

But they simply did ignore

him – but what he said was

right!

My name is Ali Baba – and I
live at 10 Downing Street,
Where Sharia Law rules the
the land – and the UK – we
did defeat!
My name is Ali Baba – and
Islam now does rule,
While Cameron, Clegg and
Osborne, all now ride a mule!

I welcome you my friends –
Ali Baba is my name –
But don't tell everyone – I
really am insane!
Little Britain is our target –
and I am the new Prime
Minister;
I welcome you to my land –
where Islam is now the

master!

My mobile phone is all free –

that is a fact –

It blends in with my religion –

plus I signed a free contract!

We all live very well – and

we have the internet –

But when we come through

your customs – we try to

"lose" the jet!

My friends, and I, would like
to say; 'We love you, the UK –
But, please, give us more of
your money – and we'll enjoy
our stay, okay?!'
We aim to tell the world about
your welfare system –
Where you give out freely to
foreign nationals – but you
hate the British Citizen!

My name is Ali Baba, and I now
have a dozen wives,
We work and breed – it is our
creed – those benefits are a
surprise!
Welcome us, you do, on the
shores of Little Britain –
Now we are in charge of you –

you Christians - you will be

regularly beaten.

My name is Ali Baba – and I

love to dance the Lambada –

But in Little Britain – I need

my umbrella!

Me and my thieving mates,

wish you all a fabulous day –

As we now are the majority –

we will enjoy our stay!

From the land of Bongo Bongo –

from the caves of Boneo.

We really are now settled in –

but we really hate the snow!

Our wives are all covered up –

and that's how it will be,

As we are now in Britain –

and we collect our money,

for free!

My name is Ali Baba – I

welcome you to Britain?

If you are of my breed –

you will be truly smitten!

Roll up, I say; 'roll up' –

for Sharia Law is here,

Now after saying all that –

I need a drink of beer!

Bless us now, oh Allah, do –

and the son of God,

No! We can't say that – Allah

is the good?

We pray for world peace –

and for all Christian's to

behave,

Or they shall all be banished —

to an Afghan cave!

My name is Ali Baba — and I

lead the UK now,

And when you all see me —

you will all saintly bow!

I thank you all for serving me —

and, please, do kiss my boss,

For we know about you

Christians — but we don't

give a toss!

Bless us holy Allah — and make

us now our dinner?

I do confess before I eat — I

have become a sinner!

My sin is worse — and it is a

curse —

But when we get our UK

welfare – we celebrate in

verse!

Thank you, oh Britain – you

make us all feel at home,

Now we are free to pillage -

and to also roam!

I really love to dance – and

gyrate to the Lambada –

If you see me in the street -

just say; 'hi, you're Eric

Estrada!'

My name is Ali Baba – and

I'm in the UK today,

Where I contact the DWP –

and gladly collect my pay!

My friend is Greedy Sinbad –

he's just told me some very

good news,

David Cameron – and Nick

Clegg – have both fallen

down some stairs!

Behold! I am the boss – of

the once proud UK,

Where me and my buddies –

all love to pray!

Please come in and join us –

but there is a very long queue;

'Where Islam is the rule – it's

sad, but very true!'

BY DARRYL ASHTON

MY NAME IS ANDREW MITCHELL

My name is Andrew Mitchell,

I was a Chief Whip, celeb,

But now my career's in ruins,

as I called a copper an alleged

PLEB!

Yes, this is true – although it

went to court,

I exchanged words with a

copper – I should have grabbed

them by the throat!

I was wheeling my bicycle –

down the Downing Street

way,

But I couldn't allow that

copper – to have the final

say!

The escapade went to court,

and then the very High Court,

Where the judge sat with

his wig on – the case he may

distort!

I had to fight for my own

reputation – and my pride

of role,

Although all the police did

say; "I should climb back in

my hole!"

I was a Parliamentary Chief

Whip – and worth a lot of

money –

But will the taxpayer pay

my legal costs – or, will my

dear old mummy?

The Downing Street elite,

we all thought we're above

the law;

"But, no we're not – not

any more – the police will

want to know!"

But, why was I pushing my

bike, and not in my posh

car?

I could have had a few more

drinks – at the "New Scotland

Yard" guest bar!

It felt so right pushing my bike –

up to the Downing Street rails,

But the next time a copper

approaches me – I'll pretend to

paint my nails!

But what have we politicians

done, to this, Little Old Britain?

When one can't say a funny

joke – as you'll get your back-

side bitten!

I found out the expensive way –

in the High Court of life,

But all it has done for me – is

cause me lots of strife!

What did I say? Why all the

fuss?

Next time round – I think I'll

use the bus!

But my crime has all been

distorted – by that copper,

who thinks they're a "CELEB" –

When in reality – they really

are a PLEB!!!!

BY DARRYL ASHTON

MY NAME IS CHARLES KENNEDY

My name is Charles

Kennedy, I do so like

a drink,

But when I'm on

Question Time – I

just cannot think!

I enjoy a little tipple –

and I smoke a fag,

But when I was on

Question Time – all

I did was nag!

I sat there like a

drunkard – bleary

eyed and sodden,

Every time I tried

to answer – my

lines, I had forgotten!
I am a proud
Scotsman — and I
like my whisky neat,
But sometimes in
the morning — I
stagger down the
street!

I was a guest on
Question Time — but
I only had some
water,
So I had a little
drinky, of whisky
and soda!
I couldn't even think
straight — I wanted
to go home —

But if I am honest –

to the pub I'd gladly

roam.

I listened to David

Dimbleby – and the

other boring' cretins –

And as I constantly

nodded off – I was

thinking; 'whisky

please!'

I couldn't stay awake

and I kept on slurring

my words –

All I wanted was

drink – not to listen

to these nerds!

I'm sat here next to

Dimbleby – I just
cannot focus now;
'I'm constantly being
nagged at – by that
silly Tory' cow!'
I have my wee flask
of whisky – ready to
drink for sure,
But if I get too drunk
they'll kick me out the
door!

So now I need a clinic –
and I'll book a room
today,
And when I'm in my
mini bar – I'll shout;
'Hip- pip...HOORAY'
But when I go in my

room – someone kicks

me on my groin –

When I turn to bop

them – I see it's...

Paul Gascoigne!

BY DARRYL ASHTON

MY NAME IS DALTON PHILIPS

My name is Dalton Philips,

and I'm the "BOSS" of the

Morrisons empire,

My job is to get things

right – and getting rich is

my desire!

I had a little office – and

a leggy' secretary,

And when we had a quiet

day – we'd embrace on

my new bed-settee!

I am the chief executive –

and what I say does go –

But recently I botched up –

our profits have been low.

I got this job I wanted –

because I knew the score,

But ever since I cocked up –

they're throwing me out

of the door!

I had a fabulous time in

charge – making myself

so rich,

But I couldn't boost the

profits more – so I'll

blame it on a glitch!

So now they are kicking

me out, because I've

failed to score;

'And now I will say goodbye –

because I can't deliver

more!'

But every time they do

recruit, a new Chief

Executive,

They always fail in their

job – will they ever

forgive?

I introduced a discount

card – to match both

Aldi and Lidl,

But everyone knows

this scheme – is just a

little fiddle?!

So, now I say; 'adios'

my friends – I leave my

job with sorrow –

I'll say; 'Good Luck to

you, dear Morrisons –

there's always a new

tomorrow.

My final word is with

regret – before you

hang by the neck;

'You could save millions

of pounds in cash, just

get rid of Ant and Dec!'

BY DARRYL ASHTON

GOODBYE TO DALTON PHILIPS

My name is Dalton Philips,

and I'm leaving Morrisons,

I couldn't do the job in

hand – I couldn't do my

sums!

Whatever did I do – to

deserve to get kicked out

of office,

When all I wanted to do –

is be a little novice?

I sat around the board table

with my fellow chums,

But all we did was talk the

talk – we just failed to do

our sums.

I knew best – well, I thought

I did – I thought I knew the score,
But then I raised the prices more – now I'm out the door!

Bradford is our base – but we'd love to relocate –
Find somewhere cheaper – before we learn our fate!
All the bosses they know best – they took their bonuses too,
But now I have cocked up – I'm heading for the loo!

Aldi is our enemy – and Lidl is so too,
But they both got it right – they knew just what to do!

We sell fruit and fresh bread –
and also fresh vegetables,
But when we hiked our
prices up – we acted like
the UNTOUCHABLES!

We cannot get it right – and
now we have to fight,
We do not want to lose our
customers – we'll hold on so
very tight!
We made mistakes – that we
know – now we all are doomed,
All our customers have gone –
now we are marooned!

We must now try harder – as
the future looks a little calm,
But, why don't we just hire –

Mr Citizen Khan!!

Goodness Gracious Me, I say;

'will someone please help us?'

I am so very sorry – to have

caused a lot of fuss!

So, goodbye to Dalton Philips,

you'll get a payoff now,

But how do you get a massive

pay-off – when you enhanced

the profits row?

Whoever does take over –

they've got to turn things

round,

Or carry on as you are – you'll

sink without a sound!

Will they recruit an American,

or a Canadian, to save this

store,

Or sell it off like Cadbury – and
make a perfect score?
Whoever does come in –
they've got their work cut out;
'Because if they fail again – the
boardroom, they will shout!'

I wish them luck, I really do –
everyone deserves a chance.
Let's hope and pray – whoever
comes in – their profits, they
can enhance.
Good luck to Morrisons, I say
that true – you will see the
light;
'And hopefully in the future,
your profits will be bright.'

BY DARRYL ASHTON

MY NAME IS DAVID CAMERON

BY DARRYL ASHTON

My name is David Cameron –

I am a very proud Tory,

But to my party colleagues –

I am a horror story.

I am the PM – of a land so

small and crowded,

But if anyone dares to

comment – they really will

be bullied.

I do have some help – but

they aren't part of my

plans,

Those Lib Dems are a waste

of space – I'll squash them

in my hands.

I've had a word with my

mate, George Osborne –

to see how we can spend

some money,

And if I have got plenty

to spend – I'll spend it on

my honey!

I do know some rich people –

and they're the friends to know;

'They are all directors of the

HSBC Bank – they can make

my money grow!'

They advise me of the tax

system – and how to avoid it,

good,

Well, I am David Cameron –

I'll fiddle my tax as I should!

I'll give them all a peerage –

as we are all corrupt –

Then I can walk around –

and feel like old King Tut!

We must keep this a secret –

our plan is all in power –

But, for goodness sake –

and to save my backside –

sack the bloody

whistleblower!

We do love our own power –

because we are all crooks;

'And when we're in a meeting –

we love to cook the books!'

Those power companies look

after us – they bung us a few

million pounds –

We all know they're all

corrupt – but, like us, they

play the money 'merry-go-

rounds!

If we win outright power –

the obese will lose their

benefits –

How dare they scrounge

their money off us – those

fatties – eating their cakes!

Their benefits I will take –

as they are just plain lazy –

Because all their money

they get paid – it really

makes me crazy.

But there is a general

election looming – and there

really is a threat –

His name is Nigel Farage –

and with UKIP – that you can

bet!

They do have many fans

now – and I am so very

concerned –

I'll have to dish up some dirt

on them all – lessons will be

learned!

I want an outright victory –

to be the Tory PM,

And kick out that Nick Clegg –

and the Lib Dems – I didn't

even want them.

But if I do win sole power –

I'll go to church and confess;

"That, I, David Cameron – will

act like Elliott Ness!"

THE GREAT TESCO FIDDLE

My name is Loadsa Money,

and I am a big boss man,

I try to make a lot of cash –

and grab even more when I

can.

I sit on the board at the

Tesco empire,

Where we all get together –

and our fiddling, we do

admire!

I do have greedy colleagues,

they are a lot like me,

We all have massive salaries –

and big bonuses for free!

We do our best to cook the

books – as we make more

cash every day;

"We come to work a four hour day – and take our fabulous pay!"

Now we got very greedy – that is very true,
But all this greed, and fiddling – we did it all for you!
My deputy is a nice fella – his name is Thieving Jerk,
He thought he'd get away with it – oh what a silly burk!

Then comes the chairman, he's a bandit too;
"He makes sure we get our

dosh – and we never have to queue!"
Then our night shift sales director – he sits down all night,
But when he does the accounts – fiddling is his delight!

We value all our customers – well, that is what we say;
"But only when they spend their money – and throw it our own way!"
We love the sounds of jingle, jingle, and smelling all that dosh,
But deep down in our hearts – we just don't give a toss!

We always say; "Every little helps", we say that all with pride,
But if the truth is known to all – we all just want to hide!
We are the big boys – that we know – and we watch our bonuses grow,
But we didn't intend to get caught – fiddling the profits more!

Now we are in trouble – but we've still got our fat pay –
But now we're classed as criminals – we all now have to pray!
We thought we were

the best – and to heck

with being honest –

All we did was cook

the books – yes, totally

dishonest!

We were the untouchables –

we milked the 'cash-flow'

system –

But now we've been caught,

it now could mean prison!

We were greedy directors –

and it was all hushed up –

But now we are exposed –

we just want to throw up!

We own Tesco Express, just

like Elliott Ness,

We were greedy bosses -

but we're now in a mess!

We felt like the mafia – we

cooked the accounting books,

Now we're all exposed as,

the elite' Tesco crooks!

We are like MPs – we lined

our own selfish pockets –

We just got too greedy – just

like the Utilities!

We are all members of the

money fiddling crew,

But now we've all been

caught – we just did it for

you!

We have all now resigned,

but we're all on full pay.

Together we all stand – and

now we all do pray.

We were Tesco bosses – so

corrupt to the core,

But we fiddled the books –

and we still wanted more!

We are all now demoted –

and quite right bleeding

too,

We even get an escort - to

the 'honest' staff loo!

We are the directors – and

we now stack the shelves

"Well, you know what we

say; "Every little helps!!!!"

A TESCO EXPRESS CHRISTMAS HUMBUG

My name is Pringle Crisp,

and I live at Tesco Express,

At the moment I'm on

special offer - but don't

tell Elliott Ness.

We hide away upon the

shelves as we're all so

very shy,

And if no one picks us

up - we all will surely

cry.

We see the lovely Lady

Sheila - and the luscious

Lady Joanna,

Then there's Lady Barbara -

three lovely ladies - you

betcha!

I see them as the tiller-

girls - working on the
tills,
But I imagine them as
"pole dancers" - giving
me some thrills!

So for all your Christmas
shopping - and all that:
'Ho! Ho! Ho!
Tesco Express is the
place to be - as Darryl
Ashton told you so.
Merry Christmas to you
all and a Happy New
Year,
So raise your glass of
Christmas cheer - and
simply enjoy a beer!!!!

But Christmas can be a

lonely time - as some

people do feel low,

But get down to Tesco

Express - where there's

lots of mistletoe!!!!

The staff are all so friendly -

and there's also free hot

punch in a mug,

But if you're an Ebenezer -

you can be a Tesco Express,

Christmas Humbug!!!!

BY DARRYL ASHTON

MY NAME IS ED MILIBAND

My name is Ed Miliband –

and I am the Labour

leader,

My job is simple – that I

know – we always enjoy

a beer!

We are the working class,

well, that's what we do

say;

'We will look after the

pennies more – just like

yesterday!'

I have a brother, David,

he's in the USA –

I beat him as labour

leader – so he just went

astray!

I enjoy a bacon sarnie,

and try to devour the

lot,

I would like to be Prime

Minister – and to stop

the rot!

When we were in power

we really overspent –

But now I promise you –

we labour will repent!

Give us a chance to be

in charge - and to be

the boss –

I know you don't trust

me – and you simply

don't give a toss!

Yes, we spent money –

and we borrowed even

more –

Now we are all suffering –

so we firmly shut the door!

We didn't curb immigration –

we allowed them all to

come in –

When people did complain –

we just played the violin!

We took no bleeding notice,

that is plain to see –

But for the poor old refugees –

everything is free!

But we do have a challenger –

and the voters love them too,

We have to fight off UKIP –

please do join the queue?

But all we do is talk – and

talk a lot of tripe,

Just like the Tory's – and the

Lib Dems – who make me

want to gripe!

I'm not like Gordon Brown,

or that flipping' Tony Blair,

They destroyed our economy,

they really didn't care.

Tony Blair was close to -

George Dubya Bush,

But deep down inside of

him – he'd like to smack

him in the mush!

They even got together –

to start an illegal war,

But all that they should

have done - is crawl back

into their lair!

We used to like the working

man – and back the unions

too,

But now when I them unions –

I just run to the nearest loo!

We really do care about our

bounty' taxpayer's cash,

So if we do get in power –

we'll just watch everything

crash!

We'll only have five years –

to line our pockets true,

And even vote ourselves a

mega pay rise; 'as we are

a thieving crew!'

BY DARRYL ASHTON

MY NAME IS FANNY MAY

My name is Fanny May

and I do feel such

dismay,

I used to be heterosexual -

but now I have turned

gay!

I used to walk around

the town - and never

wear a frown,

But now I feel so

depressed - it really gets

me down.

I used to have a husband,

we loved each other so,

But I also fancy other

women - but my husband

did not know!
I do feel so useless - as I
don't like being gay,
And what's all this nonsense,
'that same sex marriage is
okay'?

I must have upset God -
and he is now punishing
me,
But why has he made me
gay? I do so want to be
free?
The world despises me -
as a lesbian, I am now,
I used to have a handsome
husband - now I have a
cow!

I once was very normal -

not a 'hip-twirling' queer,

Why can't I be normal -

my sexuality I can steer?

All I want is my husband -

not a silly' butch woman,

I just can't accept this

'gay' business - it is a spell

that's woven!

I was so very popular -

my head was help so high,

But now I have turned gay -

all I do is cry.

I will so fight this - as in my

view it's an illness,

So many people out there -

some couldn't care less!!

I am a very proud lady -

and I want my husband

back,

I do not like being gay - I

feel I want to crack!!!!

The lord has done this to

me - well, I'll fight him all

the way,

How dare he turn me into

a gay - I will now have my

say.

I cry myself to sleep at

night - and it really gets me

down,

Why am I a queen? Do I need

to wear a crown?

I don't mind gay people - but

I do not want to join them,

I want to have my husband

back - he is a handsome gem!!

My name is Fanny May - sadly,

I am now gay.

If I repent - and pray to God -

will I be okay?

The world has gone mad - as

everyone can marry,

But in the eyes of our God, he's

turned me into a fairy!!!!

I shall hold my head up high -

that is my destiny,

To be free again is what I

need - maybe God will help

me?

I will march on - that I know -

and live my daily life,

But one day in the future, I again, will be 'husband' and 'wife'.

BY DARRYL ASHTON

MY NAME IS IAIN DUNCAN SMITH

(UK Work And Pensions Secretary)

My name is Iain Duncan

Smith, and I hate the

disabled people,

I aim to attack them

even more - I will act

like Ivan The Terrible.

I'm going to target the

poorest - and inflict so

much pain -

By stealing all their

disability benefits - this

is where I gain!

My job is to distort -

the true facts of the

sanctions, crew,

Blaming other people -
I'll tell them what to
do?
We thrive on being
bullies - as the
vulnerable we do
target,
Our reforms are not
popular - but I'll just
smoke my cigarette!

I am not a very nice
person - and I really
don't give a fig,
But my aim is to really
bully - the disabled's
graves, they all can
dig.
Even if they're

genuine, and really
badly disabled,
I couldn't give a
monkeys - new
sanctions I will table.

I am part of a Tory
tosser group, and we
really don't give a damn,
Even if our welfare
reforms - really are a
sham!
The bleeding hearts
we'll ignore - and the
tears will all start
flowing -
Bring on the disabled
people - I want to see
them all cowering?

My name is Iain Duncan

Smith - and I really am

so hated,

But it gives me fantastic

pleasure - to see those

benefits confiscated.

I'll suck up to the PM -

and I'll get a lovely peer;

'When the rightful thing

I really should do - is

jump off a Blackpool pier!!!!'

BY DARRYL ASHTON

MY NAME IS MEATY MUSLIM

My name is Meaty Muslim,

and I love a sausage roll,

Any meat will do me -

but they're always so very

small!

They really are so tasty,

but they've shrunk, as over

might,

And they are too quick

to eat - they're gone in

just one bite!

But now there is an issue -

we Muslims are offended?

They're full of Christian

meat - tasty pork has now

descended!

The PC brigade are causing strife - just like they always do;
'But every time I go and buy one - there's always a very long queue!'

I also like my meatballs, especially in rich gravy.
Those tasty meatballs are delicious - they send the Muslims crazy!!!!
There is also the tasty pasty, all covered in OXO sauce,
Tasty, meaty, and exotic - I'll have to have one of those!

So welcome to my shop -
you Muslims' I do say,
'Come and buy your
sausage rolls - there is
plenty to buy today?
Take no notice of the PC
people - they are an
annoying crew,
But if they keep sticking
their oars in - I'll drown
them all in a stew!

BY DARRYL ASHTON

MY NAME IS MUCKY BUM JACKSON

My name is Mucky Bum

Jackson - and I want

to be an MP,

I get to choose my

toilet paper - and I'll

decorate my Christmas

tree.

You see, I really don't

like Christmas - I am a

proud' Bah Humbug,

I'll go to church and

say a prayer - and get

the Muslim bug!!!!

I have to start a protest,

to save Christianity,

But hail the Muslim

brotherhood - for all

eternity!

I will kick out David

Cameron - from his

10 Downing Street,

home,

And refurbish it into

a mosque - and make

it a pleasure dome!!!!

Then I will be PM -

and claim my sanctuary -

Then join the Muslim

brotherhood - and start

world war three!!!!

Then I'll change the

house of commons -

now that will be a treat,

Then I'll sit down with

my bearded friends -

swatting flies as they

speak!!!!

Oh, hail, the Muslim

takeover - we now

have the power,

We'll build more

Mosques for our mates,

and cleans our souls

in the shower!!!!

The Britain we used

to know - is now all

dead and gone,

Now for Iain Duncan

Smith - where did I

put my gun?

The future of Little

Britain, is ours to

really celebrate,

We hail all the Muslim

faith - but, Christianity,

we do hate.

So, welcome to the UK -

as we say a prayer

to Allah' population;

'Be prepared to meet

the new PM: 'Mr Mucky

Bum Jackson!!!!'

BY DARRYL ASHTON

MY NAME IS NICK CLEGG

My name is Nick Clegg

and I am the Deputy PM,

No matter what I say – I

am always not to blame.

My party are the Lib Dems –

and we're hoping to win

some votes,

But I dare not look at the

odds – in case it really

chokes!

I once had a TV debate

about the UK immigration –

Competing against Nigel

Farage – he won the

hearts of the nation.

I spoke a load of bull –
well, what did you all
expect?
When I stood next to
the UKIP leader – he
really was select!

I am in a coalition – but
I hate those Tory jerks,
Me and my Lib Dem
cronies – really want
more perks!

We want to win the
election – that is our
aim,
The new PM I aim to
be- Nick Clegg is my
name!

I know we are a long

shot – and that's what

the poles do show,

But if I promise to cut

taxes – the rich will

surely know.

I feel like Charles

Kennedy, wanting a

little scotch –

It must block out the

pain of losing – which

happens oh so much!

I do want to help the

disabled more – to cut

their welfare more,

By taking more of their

welfare benefits – and

helping the rich to score!

My name is Nick Clegg –

and now I'm like a Tory,

Cos when it comes to my

conference speech;

It'll be just like... Jackanory!

BY DARRYL ASHTON

MY NAME IS NIGEL FARAGE

My name is Nigel Farage,

I am the leader of UKIP –

I have been on Channel 4

TV– but the truth they

did let slip.

Yes, I like to smoke – and

I enjoy a few beers,

And when I tour the UK –

everybody cheers!

Some say we are racists –

I strongly disagree.

But foreign nationals are

pouring in – and get

everything for free!

I have an Asian woman –

she is a rising star,

She's sorting out our mass
immigration – she will go
really far.

All I want is our country
back – and to exit the EU –
They only cater for the
corrupt MEP's – not the
likes of me and you!
I had my doubts and my
concerns – about being
on camera –
All Channel 4 have really
done – is create more
propaganda.
We want to sort out the
immigration – is that such
a crime?
We are the ones to sort it –

as we will make the time.

Labour have failed badly –

and so have the Tory's too –

And as for the Coalition lot –

they belong in one big stew!

All I want are controlled

borders – and to check who

shouldn't be here –

Then we can deport the ones –

am I crystal clear?

We are NOT against those

immigrants – who want to

really work,

And contribute to our

economy – and not intend

to shirk.

We have to be realistic – we

are a small island –

But all those genuine folk –
we'll give them a helping
hand.

Please? Do come in? We do
welcome you to Britain –

All that we ask of you – is to
learn English – and be an
inspiration!

So, I urge you to vote for
UKIP – and let us make
Britain great,

Let's get rid of Cameron –
his policies we all do hate.

I could, however, do a
deal – with Labour's'
Miliband –

And get together and talk

some sense – and find out

just were we all stand?

UKIP are not anti-Europe –

as we are all branded;

'All the lies that the party's

say about us – are all very

one sided.'

We must reclaim our

borders – and help the UK

to prosper –

Then when we've got our

UK back – we can run the

country proper!!

Yes, folks, we can do it – and

power can be mine.

UKIP will always reign – and

grow stronger in good time.

My name is Nigel Farage –

I am the new PM,

Now I'm in 10 Downing Street –

now I'll surely show them!!

THE END

MY NAME IS PRICKLY BOTTOM

My name is Prickly Bottom,

I reside in the House of

Lords.

I visit every other day - and

still get paid loads.

We live on another world -

and we are always on the

make,

Even in the restaurant - I

do enjoy free cake.

We sit high in the chambers -

and we sometime's fall asleep.

But the speaker does soon

wake us - he's just Little Bo

Peep!

We all have our mobile phones -

and tablets by the score,

And when we do all fall asleep -

you can hear an almighty

snore!!!!

You see, we are all very old -

and we sit and look so busy,

Nodding our heads up and down,

it gets us in a tizzy!

Some of the women too - are also

very craggy,

They sit there flashing their open

pins - and looking oh so saggy!!

Anyone can get voted in - just

bung a healthy donation,

David Cameron will be pleased,

he'll create a Tory-infested nation!!!!

Roll up! Roll up! And welcome to

the house of sin,

Where you can go in the bar - and

help yourself to a gin!

The House of Lords, is an asylum

place - which Sir Guy Fawkes is

now eyeing up.

He's all set to fly in first class —

and blow the buggers up!

My name was Prickly Bottom -

but the smoke and fire has

changed that,

I am now called; 'Scorched

Bottom, and I feel like Basil the

rat!!!!'

BY DARRYL ASHTON

MY NAME IS SIR GUY FAWKES

My name is Sir Guy Fawkes,

and I am now coming back,

I aim to blow up parliament -

this deed, I will now crack.

My mission is so simple - to

destroy all UK MPs.

Make them all really suffer -

bring them to their knees.

I aim to rid the UK of the

corruption in high places,

Starting with those MPs -

all have got two faces!

To destroy David Cameron -

and Iain Duncan Smith,

Then I can celebrate - my

cigar I shall proudly sniff.

I plan is now in motion - I
will now achieve my goal,
Watching those MPs flirt -
then I'll watch them crawl.
I've recruited some more
terrorists - they were known
as refugees.
They came in via Germany -
apparently with ease!

The UK are very welcoming -
so we must now show our
thanks,
By blowing up the parliament -
and sending in the tanks!
I sit down in the cellar - with
a lovely bunch of misfits,
Asylum seekers saying their

thanks - our happy mood now
lifts.

The people of the UK - are now
so dissolutioned -
The Christian country we used
to be - has now been completely
siphoned.
I see the future for the UK - as
a miserable Muslim state,
So I shall now light the fuse -
and seal the UK's fate!!

I will now bomb the parliament -
and get rid of the houses of
corruption -
To bring the peace and happiness
back - and STOP the Muslim
invasion.

The fuse is lit - as the naked

flame burns - the target - the

barrels of gunpowder,

As I leave the doomed building -

I turn and feel a shudder!

As I ride away upon my horse,

the building does explode;

'The heavenly sight I see so

clear - as I rest in my new abode.'

The refugees who assisted me -

have all been well rewarded,

They have been granted asylum -

while parliament exploded!!!!

Hail! Hail! The parliament is gone,

and so are all MPs.

I really was successful - I brought

them to their knees.

Remember! Remember! This night

forever - when parliament finally

chokes;

For my name will be a living legend,

as the infamous...Sir Guy Fawkes!!!!

BY DARRYL ASHTON

MY NAME IS TAX AVOIDANCE

My name is Tax Avoidance,

and I work for a well known

bank,

I help most customers to

avoid paying tax – and with

their money, they all do

thank.

I am the leader of a shifty

crew – and have friends in

very high places,

We love to make millions

of pounds – we are the

corrupt aces!

We could be the

Untouchables, just like Al

Capone,

And avoid paying any tax

at all – more interest I will

own.

We are in this together –

and certain MPs too –

We enjoy being on the

fiddle – we are a crooked

crew!

I sit is my plush office –

with shag-pile carpet

on the floor –

My aim is to fiddle my

taxes – tax avoidance I

just adore!

The taxpayers of the UK

will surely bail us out —

We are in this all together,

but I'm the one with clout!

We do have a board

meeting — once every week,

To decide how much tax

to withhold — we have a

bloody cheek!

I sit on my bottom all day —

just counting all my money,

And call for my leggy

secretary, she is my tax-

dodging honey!!

I have to look after the

boys, and act so innocent,

Getting caught we cannot

do – I'm conducting an experiment!!

Yes, we love to cook the
tax books – and we really,
help ourselves,
So we can all screw our
profits system – just like
troubled Tesco – well,
'every little helps!'

I said I felt like Al Capone,
fiddling all my taxes – but
now I'm in a mess,
But a bloody interfering
bank clerk brought us all
crashing down – his name?
it was Elliott Ness!!!!

BY DARRYL ASHTON

THE DASTARDLY GUY FAWKES

I can hear the potential

corpses, shouting up

above –

While I sit here in my

lair, lurking in my cove.

The air is dank and very

cold,

But the fuse is ready –

so behold?

I glare at the gigantic

barrels, of gunpowder,

for my use,

And just to see it looking

at me – will I call a truce?

My dastardly plot is right

on track – to blow the

building sky high,

I visualise this moment

of mine – this I can't deny.

I'll teach those scum not

to laugh – they shall be

blown to bits,

But, oh, god in heaven –

my legs just do the splits!

History is mine in the making

– my name is Guy Fawkes,

I will be remembered for

laughing - as the elite all

painfully chokes.

I gather up my thoughts

and clutch my bottle of

wine,

Well, being here in a

stinking cellar – I have to

pass the time!

Looking oh so ghoulish,

as my heart does beat

so fast,

Soon I will light the fuse –

history at last!

I must think of the future,

as I delve into madness,

Sitting here in this stinking

pit – it causes sheer sadness.

But, behold! Wait? I hear

sounds of soldiers, and

they're so very near,

I must light this bloody fuse;

'then no more to fear!'

Trying to hold the fuse I

do – and with a shaky

hand,

Blast them all to the deaths

of hell – and a plague across

the land!

Bloody rats are everywhere,

I need to work so fast,

Then before the rats get me –

I'll cause a mighty blast?

The future of the English

Parliament, hangs now

with me –

Ready to change the

history – I'll do it all with

glee!

I wish I'd gone on Ebay –

or Amazon.com,

Then I could have bought

myself a lovely bottle of

rum!

But this is the future of

the world - in years ahead

will arrive,

But when I light this bloody

fuse, no one will survive!

One day my name will be

history – as like Parliament,

I shall prosper,

And then my spirit will live

on, in that gothic...house of

usher!

But now my friends, I tell

you this – with a candle

burning;

'I will now light the fuse,

my stomach now is churning.'

There they go – up in smoke,

oh, what a fabulous sight,

As parliament falls to the

ground – I now shall say; '

goodnight!'

My deed now is done, my

name is now in history,

And every year on this day,

the people all do burn me!

I would have met the queen,

and got a royal pardon,

But I was promptly executed...

within the royal garden!

BY DARRYL ASHTON

THE FALL OF THE HOUSES OF PARLIAMENT

Trick or treat the MPs cry,

We want more money –

our pockets are dry.

We are all greedy – you all

know that's true,

We want more expenses –

as we now jump the queue!

Trick or treat the gravy

train is here,

We enjoy the ride – and

give a big cheer.

To Brussels we go – filling

our pockets –

And as its Halloween – we

act like muppets.

Trick or treat Westminster

will fall –

Sir Guy Fawkes will come

back – as he hears our call.

The zombies in Parliament,

are the walking dead,

And this will come true – it

has to be said!

Trick or treat it is Halloween,

The MPs in Parliament swear

never to be seen.

How right they are my ghoulish

friends,

Exterminate them all – and set

new trends!

Trick or treat I can smell smoke,

As the Parliament burns – MPs

do choke.

The house of corruption falls to the ground,

Sir Guy Fawkes, in spirit, at last is found.

Trick or treat there's silence all around,

The fall of the Parliament does astound.

The house of horrors is now all dust,

Now happy times will follow – and that is a must!

Trick or treat the UK shout,

Freedom is here – there is no doubt.

Sir Guy Fawkes has done it - as he takes some refreshment -

As we all do cheer; "The Fall

of The Houses of Parliament!"

BY DARRYL ASHTON

WE ARE THE TORY TOSSPOTS

We are the Tory Tosspots,

we love to rob the poor,

We have promised some

more tax cuts – being rich

we do adore.

We want to help the better

off – as they'll donate to

us –

But those lower-class

scrimpers – they just cause

us a lot of fuss.

We have to be ready – for

the people's party now,

But we haven't a chance in

hell – because UKIP folk do

bow.

We also make more

promises – and spout out

yet more lies,

And when we are exposed

as liars – we'll just hire a few

more spies!

We care about immigration –

well, that is what we say;

But everyone can still come

in – and cause mass disarray!

We promise to end those

human rights – and make

our country great –

But if UKIP do get their way –

they'll firmly shut the gate!

We are the Tory Tosspots –
and we hate those coalition
twerps,
Every time I see Nick Clegg –
he sucks' like his party of
jerks!

Osborne too, and his Eton
crew – they rally round the
rich –
But when Clegg sees Theresa
May – he calls her a silly bitch!

The Tory Tosspots are almost
dead – and Ukip will come in;
'Because voting for those Tory
Tosspots – it really is a sin!'

BY DARRYL ASHTON

WE ARE THE UK TORY GOVERNMENT

My name is David Cameron,

and I love the working class –

All my colleagues know me;

'as I talk out of my ass!'

We sit around a table – all

feeling miserable,

Knowing that the future –

looks so bleeding terrible!

My name is David Cameron –

I am still in very deep shock;

'My Mrs loves me so very

much – because I like to

wear a frock!'

We are to help the disabled –

by bullying them even more,

And stealing all their benefits –

I simply do adore.

We are the Tory party – and
we love the super rich –
We always take donations –
and never ever snitch!
The bankers are our friends –
as they caused a credit crunch,
But how do I say; 'thank you' –
we all go out for lunch!

We caused a mass conspiracy,
at the recent general election –
Labour actually won it – on a
close up second inspection.
Everyone voted labour – so we
Tories all took note;
'We rigged the election votes
in secret – and we easily won

the vote!'

We were worried about that UKIP – we saw them as a threat,
But we smeared them all the way – something they won't ever forget!
We couldn't handle Nigel Farage – he spoke a lot of sense –
He always gives direct answers – in his own elite defence.

UKIP were the party to sort out immigration –
They always were so honest – they were the voters salvation.

We couldn't handle that — so
we called them all racist —
But deep down in our hearts
we know; 'their racism didn't
exist.'

We are the Tory party — and
we have power for five more
years —
By the time we have all
finished — the UK will be in
tears.
But we do not give a damn —
as we are all millionaires —
We'll wreck this, the UK —
and then we'll all shout...
CHEERS!!!!

We're for the working people —

well, that is what we say;

'To take more tax from your

wages, it'll be a fabulous day!'

We are the Tory party – we'll

look after you so well,

As for all those disabled people –

well, they can all go to hell!!

BY DARRYL ASHTON

WE ARE THE BOYS IN THE BOARDROOM!!!!!!

We are the boys in the
boardroom, and we talk
a lot of tosh,
But when it comes to our
bonuses - we get a lot
of dosh!

We always like to fiddle -
well, that is in our blood;
'To award ourselves mass
bonuses - like we know
we should.'

But recently there's been
some changes - we've
allowed two women on
the board,

And when they flash their shapely legs - we are never ever bored!!

We love to enhance our profits - and to manipulate the books,
Because deep on down in our blood - we're just a bunch of CROOKS!!

I cannot name our company, for all I say is true,
All the boys on the board - are bent like a sailor's crew!!

But when we're round our table - discussing feeble things,

We glance at the ladies

underwear - their knickers

and their strings!!

Sometime's we are called

sexist - but that's just office

banter,

But when a lady shows their

pins - we often do all tease

her.

We are the lads of the board -

and our job is very cushy,

But having these two ladies

here - oh they are openly

smutty!!

We aim to please at the board,

as our fellowship does grow,

But how do we get away with things; 'oh, wouldn't you all like to know!!'

Sexist banter is the game - as the office is our place,
And chatting up the ladies - is always done with grace!!!!

So now you know we love to fiddle - as sometime's we get bored,
But this is just a little perk - but now I have just scored!!!!

BY DARRYL ASHTON

THE LITTLE PUNKS...AND THE SELLOTAPE TEACHER!!!!!!

I'll sellotape your mouth

shut, you noisy little child,

I am the teacher – and I'm

known to be wild.

How dare you rule my

classroom, you horrible

little git –

Now where's my sellotape –

to seal your mouth, you

horrible little twit?

Oh, isn't it cruel? The

headmaster doesn't

approve?

Well sod the lot of them –

I'm feeling in the groove!

We mustn't touch the little sods, that isn't the school rules,
But I dare you step in my class – you horrible little fools!

If you speak out of line – or are naughty in any way,
I'll make you wish you weren't here, I will make your day!
When I tell you to be quiet, that is what you do,
Or you little punks – it's the sellotape, too true!

So I've been suspended, I really don't give a toss,

To hell with all them do-

gooders, and the bloody

boss!

Those little punks, called;

"children" – are sometimes

a real pain,

But when I get my sellotape,

out – I'll do it all again!

BY DARRYL ASHTON

SUGAR! SUGAR!

WE ALL DO LOVE YOU!

Sugar, sugar, how are you?
I'm not very well, my days
are through!
"What do you mean, your
days are through?"
"I'm going to ba banned –
by the do-gooding crew!"

"But, why is that, you are
so sweet,
You make people feel good –
you are a treat!"
The government says; "I'm
bad, as I make people fat,
Oh, I don't know; "it's just
tit for tat!"

"Yes, I know that – but why

do they bully me?

Some people like sugar –

especially in their tea!"

"Please don't worry, I do

have a friend,

He's called Salt – and he's

all the trend!"

"Come with me, my sweet

sugared friend,

We'll have some cereal –

and start a new sugary trend?

Ignore the scaremongers –

they aren't so sweet –

They'll ban everything –

including fresh meat!"

"What shall we do, I do love

my sugar?"

"Just ignore them – we do

have each other!"

So both salt and sugar – lived

happily together,

Straight in the mouths of us

all, forever!

BY DARRYL ASHTON

TWO LITTLE TROUBLED DOLLS

I know two little dolls,

and both are very cute,

They both lay around all

day long – and one is up

the chute!

Their colour has caused

an outrage – because of

racial law,

One is white – the other

is brown – so now there

is uproar!

The dolls are not now

happy – and who can

really blame them?

So now the dolls break

wind – and cause a

smelly mayhem!
These dolls are victims
of racism madness,
And all these dolls did
really want – is to live
in total happiness?

The dolls are looking
bemused – as their skin
colour is so different -
There's nothing wrong
with being brown – they
laugh and seize the
moment!
They have a loving home,
my friends - and they love
the people who care,
Their home is at ARGOS –
their love they do share.

But, sadly, there is now

trouble – and their skin

colour is to blame –

It's only those bloody

humans – playing the

silly race game!

The dolls are not happy –

so they decide to fight

back,

"Please leave our skin

colour alone – or you'll

get us both the sack?"

The dolls do battle with

the race squad – and

the dolls tell them to

stop their madness;

"Do not insult our skin

colour – just show us

some more kindness?"

Your problem is in your

minds – you humans

are really sad;

'So stop all this racial

rubbish – and make us

dolls feel glad?'

Let us live our daily

lives – and eat our

farleys rusks –

And put an end to all

this squabbling – as

it really, really, sucks.

So, when we hear

this racial madness –

being targeted at us –

It makes us fill our

nappies – because of

all the fuss!

So I am white – my

friend is brown – is it

really worth a frown?

So one nice dolly

admires their tan – and

loves their golden

brown!

We'd like to say a thank

you – to Argos, who

gave us a home,

So if you'll get your

money out – to Argos,

you will roam!

BY DARRYL ASHTON

TWO-FACED HYPOCRITES...NOW DO YOU ALL UNDERSTAND????!!!!

We seem to have two
faces - well, most of
us seem to do -
We seem to say things
in a nice way - even
when not true!
"Oh, what a lovely
person - they lit up
every room,
They always had a
smile for you - even
when in doom?"

They are now dead -
so we praise them
more and more,

But when they were

still alive - we hated

them for sure!!

We always show our

true colours - when

someone dies,

We praise them all

the more - why is

this not a surprise?

'What a fabulous

fella' - or, 'what a

lovely lady',

You say you will

miss them - inside

your laughing like

crazy!!!!'

We are very good

actors - and we

always praise the

dead,

We never praise

the living - we

should do this

more instead.

It really is a

tragedy, that we

seem to act this

way,

Being two-faced

hypocrites - is how

it makes their day!!!!

To praise a person

in their death - who

you really couldn't

stand -

We sometimes are

two-faced hypocrites -

now do you all

understand????!!!!

BY DARRYL ASHTON

THE REAL HOUSES OF PARLIAMENT...
ON QUEER SQUARE

In the Houses of Parliament,

there are some queer folk,

all they do is nod their heads,

and talk a very good talk!

The Houses of Parliament

is corrupt - they seem to like

their work,

But every time it shows them

on TV - all they do is shirk!

They're tapping on their

tablets as though they are all

bored,

They turn up in their suits -

and even get full board!

They claim their expenses,

like any other person,

But not like me and you -

they don't have any good

reason!

The Houses of Parliament,

is know for its diversity,

Every one in there - has ben

to university!

They employ all their relatives -

and keep it in the family,

They pay them cash in the

hand - dodging the tax man

superbly!

The Houses of Parliament -

as a history of such slender,

You can yourself join this

club - but one has to be a

bender!

This house is based in

London Town - were there's

hardly any cockneys,

But there is a club so

exclusive - and it attracts

lots of willies!!!!

The Houses of shame - is

were the MPs all gather,

Fiddling more of their cash -

they're all in it together!!!!

Lord Gay, meet Lord Bender,

whatever has gone wrong?

Everyone has got a title -

watch out for a song!!!!

The Houses of Parliament,

is the home on Queer Square,

Where all the MPs congregate -

lurking in their lair!!

So may I welcome - a special guest so new,

His name is Sir Guy Fawkes - he's returned just for you!

He will now clean up this place - and then he'll be a knight.

He's set to blow the lot up - to the cheering crowd's delight.

The Houses of the Parliament, is finally laid to rest,

Goodbye to the Parliament on Queer Square, now we feel such zest!!!!

A new day has now dawned

as all the UK is free.

Freedom from these parasites,

is happiness to you and me.

The Houses are no more - as

history is now made,

But why do all gay MPs - like

their carpet laid!!!!

BY DARRYL ASHTON

MY NAME IS SWING HIGH FLAG

My name is Swing High Flag,

and don't the police just nag?

I was walking on the pavement -

waving my Union Jack Flag,

A group of police came up to

me - glaring their teeth so

well,

And carted me off to the police

station - and put me through

sheer hell.

I asked them what my crime was -

and they started just to giggle,

I really was so furious - to be

piggy in the middle!

The cops said; 'I offended people -

well, that was news to me,

All the people who saw me -

were swinging their ISIS and

free!!!!'

What the heck has happened -

when you cannot wave a flag,

Especially praising your country -

as the police ride in their jag?

The terrorists are free - to wave

their offensive slogan,

The ISIS flag is NOT welcome -

they seem to be outspoken!

All I do for Queen and country -

I proudly wave my pride,

No, not my little golly friend,

he I must now hide!!!!

So welcome to Little Britain -

were our traditions are being

eroded,

And all those people all flood in - and bring their guns all loaded?

The police have got their priorities wrong - but that is nothing new,
They simply ignore those scum bags - their terror they do spew.
Attack the good - and ignore the bad - that is the British way,
It really is little wonder when we see the cops - we feel so much dismay!!!!

So lets all be proud and wave our pride - and make our

country great?

Then we can live in peace

and harmony - that we can

all create?

So boo hoo to the PC police -

and if they start to nag,

And if they ask you for your

name - just say your; 'Swing

High Flag!!!!'

BY DARRYL ASHTON

WE ARE THE BLACKPOOL COUNCILLORS

(Featuring Hollywood Movie Director TIM BURTON)

We are the Blackpool

councillors, we are

the elite you see,

Tim Burton's turning

the lights on - because

he paid us a fee!

We licked his Yankee

shoes - to this he was

so thankful,

Then he paid us one

million - it really is

plentiful!!

He also disrupted the

town - and the people

were not happy,

But we got paid one
million - we had to
disrupt the elderly.
We sit in our posh
chambers - all rich
and prosperous too,
When we take back-
handers - we are in
front of the queue!!!!

We only have members,
who can pull some
strings of shame,
But we always pass
the buck, of course,
we cannot take the
blame!!!!
Tim Burton paid us
generously, a cool

one million pounds,
We shoved it in our
bank accounts - of
course, on corrupt
grounds!!!!

The grand life of us
councillors, is like
the corrupt MPs,
We always claim
our expenses -
especially our
massive fees!!!!
Look after number
one - is our motto
as we go,
Collecting a massive
pension - if we're
ever shown the door!!

We are on the board

of willies - and I've

got my whisky flask,

The men are very

kinky, they like to

wear a basque!!!!

The bosses are all

forbidden - to be

honest in any way;

'Scratching the

backsides of the rich -

it has to be this way!!!!'

So welcome to Tim

Burton - the Yankee

film director,

Switching on the

illuminations - the

fee is the protector!!!!

The lights are dazzling,

and everyone's happy -

and the council are

all there,

Rubbing shoulders

with Tim Burton - as

they crawl back in to

their lair!

BY DARRYL ASHTON

MILKING ONES UDDER - WE ARE THE BIG FAT MILK COWS

I am a great big fat

milk cow, and my

udder is really full,

I'm eating lots of

grass - my udder,

they do pull!

The farmer's up

real early - to milk

us all today,

And all the tasty

milk we give - will

make our chocolate'

Milk Tray!

The government all

talk tough - and the

supermarkets also

rob us -

We are the big fat

milk cows - and we

hate all this fuss.

Our farmer's need a

decent wage - as

they supply the milk,

It really tastes so

very nice - just like

silky silk!

We are the big fat

milk cows - who

walk around in the

field,

Grazing on all the

grass - wearing our

protective shield.

We love our dairy

farmers - but they
need to earn a living;
'But, the poor and
skint farmers - the
supermarkets are
all busy shafting!!!!'

People love their
milk - in their tea
or coffee, too -
Even on their
Weetabix, milk is
good for you.
We are the big fat
milk cows - we
invade the stores
today,
We'll make our
concerns known -

to give our farmers

decent pay.

Now if the stores

don't listen, or you

try to pull the wool -

We, the big fat milk

cows - will send a

ballistic mad BULL!!!!

Now this will be the

last resort - as our

bully isn't tame,

But he will make

you all see sense -

and that's our biggest

aim.

So please don't pull

the "udder" one - as

the farmers are all

now struggling;

'All the low, low prices -

the farmer's, they

are killing!!!!'

We are the big fat

milk cows - crusading

for our bosses,

Let's give our farmers

a decent wage - and

help to stop their

losses?

BY DARRYL ASHTON

A PARASITE IN THE WATER-FEATURING DAVID CAMERON

(Featuring both United Utilities and PM David Cameron)

A parasite in the water -

is swimming in disguise,

Courtesy of United Utilities,

it's sore upon the eyes!

What the heck has gone

wrong - for a parasite to

swim?

I think I'll flush it out -

and use the power of

Vim!!!!

A parasite is in the water -

what will we all do?

Just take a shower - and

hold your breath - the

parasite will find you?
Upon the beach they all
do lurk - some wear a
medallion.
The parasite in the water -
is identified as David
Cameron!!!!

There's a parasite in the
water - the fish have
swum away.
The PM David Cameron -
is sure to go astray!
He's lurking in the water -
the fish decide to bite,
But the parasite in the
water - really tastes of
sh*te!!!!

United Utilities are now

very worried, they are

set to kill this parasite,

Just call on the piranha

fish - they will come and

bite?

The parasite in the water,

is travelling around the

Europe,

But every now and again -

he has to replace his

stirrup?

The compensation is now

being counted - for 'dog

poo' is to blame.

The parasite in the water -

really has no shame!!!!

So, please, United Utilities,

do us all a favour,

When you kill the parasite

in the water - make sure

it is forever!

BY Darryl Ashton

MERRY CHRISTMAS FROM ALEKSANDR ORLOV - SERGEI AND OLEG

Come along, Sergei, we

have to go to Morrisons,

They have lots of

Christmas goodies - and

chocolate sensations!

But I want to buy some

mongoose meat and

some very tasty steak,

But when I see the prices -

surely it is a mistake!

I cannot pay that - and

Sergei has no money,

But recently I do admit -

he's turned a little bit

funny.

I do not like this Black Friday shopping - the humans are acting all silly,
They run around like old Sergei - and they are also very lippy!!

Sergei wants a new computer - for his IT department -
But if I don't buy him one - it causes massive argument!

We even tried Tesco Express - but they are far too dear,

They always say; 'Merry
Christmas' - but their
prices we all do fear!

Oleg is coming to see
us - for a holiday -
But, if I'm really honest -
he causes much dismay!

But we all do meet together,
in my big posh mansion,
Well, even in Meerkovo -
we celebrate Christmas
season!
But I never got my tasty
steak - so now I play
with my furry pimple,
Who said Christmas was
happy - I now feel so

simple!

Sergei might get poorly -
as he eats a lot of jelly,
But every Christmas it is
always the same - Sergei
gets a fat belly!!!!

Now we have had enough,
and we are going home,
On our way to Meerkovo -
where we will all roam.

We have been very busy -
in the Hollywood Super
Movies,
And both me and Sergei -
we act like a couple of
smoothies!!!!

Merry Christmas to you
all - as Sergei plays with
his furry pimple -
Happy New Year, I say to
you - let's hope it's all so
SIMPLE!!!!

BY DARRYL ASHTON

ALEKSANDR ORLOV AND SERGEI GO TO SYRIA

My name is Aleksandr Orlov,

founder of meerkat empire,

But I feel so very troubles -

as Sergei's treading the wire!

He wants to go to Syria? To

help kill all the terrorists -

I tell him; 'Sergei, you need

some support - you can't

take any risks!'

So now we charter super

furry jet - complete with

new meerkat' sat-nav,

To help us to get to Syria -

Sergei's brain is naff!!

So, we are now on our

way - and feel like the

expendables,

I don't know about feeling

like the expendables - we

seem to lose our marbles!!!!

But now we touch down -

it is very warm and sandy,

But me and faithful Sergei -

have meerkat guns all

ready.

We will fight and destroy -

those ISIS cowardly terrorists,

But when we hide behind

the stone - Sergei eats

his crisps!!!!

Sergei? I shout quite loudish,

we have to be professional,

We have to destroy these

killers - and then run over

the hill!!!!

We have our meerkat guns

all ready - and I see a wall

of rats,

Oh, my, son of a mongoose,

we have more supportive

meerkats!!!!

Onward we go - in for the

kill, as we kick the terrorists

poison,

But why is Sergei screaming

loud - he's been shot in his

furry bottom!!!!

But he gets up - all heroic -

and before he does forget,

We have to defeat the ISIS -

and jump back on super

meerkat jet!!!!

Sergei is on the field - and

his claws are all intact,

Then he kicks the ISIS

backsides - Sergei uses

his tact!!!!

We have won the war - the

meerkat is victorious,

But why do the humans

always kick-up - and make

lots of fuss?

Now we head off home -

to play on computermabob,

But Sergei's eating crisps

again - he's now a little slob!!

We have destroyed the ISIS

cretins - and Sergei plays

with his furry pimple -

When we return as the

heroes - because it was so...

SIMPLE!!!!!!

BY DARRYL ASHTON

A DAY WITH ALEKSANDR ORLOV

I'm sitting in my study

pruning my little claws,

I have to look professional –

especially when I'm in

doors.

We are having a party –

as Sergei needs a break,

As all he constantly does

all day is mope around

and squeak!

He has been very poorly,

and he's been in hospital,

I had to work the

computermables – because

Sergei was too ill!

He even joined a circus –

and he dressed as a clown,

He is too good for that –

but he always wears a frown!

He is so very old and grey,

and coming close to

retirement,

He should take things easy,

not cause an argument!

But Sergei does work hard –

all day and all night long,

And he also makes my

meals for me, and bangs

the dinner gong!

I have to sit more

comfortables, I have to

be professional,

I cannot lift a claw to

help – I have to be

rational!

Now we have a house

guest – a little baby

meerkat –

Baby Oleg meerkat –

but he's getting very

fat!

He came to us so

suddenly, in a little

basket,

And Sergei is now a

nanny – I won't let

him forget it.

Sergei works so hard –
he cooks, cleans and
makes me drinks of
tea –
He also is in charge of,
the Meerkat IT!

My days are very busy –
I prune my fur all day;
'Because being very
famous – we sometime's
have guests to stay.'

Then we have a disco –
and dance like Meerkat
Presley –
But recently Sergei has
acquired ; 'a real meerkat

skittle belly!'

I like to watch the TV news,
but it's always doom and
gloom,
But Oleg and Sergei are
always playing – I can hear
them in my room.

We are playing trick or treat,
and Sergei is a vampire,
Baby Oleg is a witch – oh you
have to admire!

My Gothic mansion is the
setting, for Aleksandr Dracula,
Because I will spit meerkat
blood – at the mongoose in
particular!

We are in the Hollywood

Movies – and annoying

the Terminator.

But Sergei wants to go

to Africa – and swim with

an alligator!!

We will go to Africa – and

collect Baby Oleg,

Just as Sergei feels better –

he hurt his furry leg!!

We will one day return

home – to my big posh

mansion house,

And Oleg will run around –

chasing a little mouse.

We seem to be on an

adventure – travelling

around the world.

And Sergei making rice

pudding – but he made

it – and it curled!!

We really have to go now –

as our bedtime is now here,

But Sergei has been

working hard – and he's

drinking meerkat beer!!!!

I shall drink Champagne –

and tickle Sergei's nipple,

When we wake up tomorrow –

everything will be SIMPLE!!!!

So, farewell, my friends – till

we meet again,

Sergei is so manic – I think

he is insane!!

Off to bed we go – but why

does Sergei always snore?

But I soon kick him out of

bed – and he loudly hits

the floor!!

BY DARRYL ASHTON

GOOD GOD AND ALLAH BOTH DO RULE THE SHORES

Allah said to Good God:

'I'm really quite cheesed

off,'

Good God said to Allah:

'Yes, I too feel a little

ruff'.

"What is wrong with

the crazy human people?

All they do is hurt and

kill each other - and

shoot at my own temple?"

'There has to be a

reason - they call it

terrorism -

Always killing one

another - and for no

good reason!'

'The world was a better

place - when Moses

was at large,

He parted the sea of

life - as the peasants

all did charge.'

Good God said: 'I do

agree with you - and

I will now make some

changes,

I'll put the living fear

in all of them - I'll

report them all as

crazies!!!!'

'I aim to be the boss -

and I'll put Samson on

red alert,

He can then destroy

the world - and then

they'll feel the hurt?'

'What about the UK MPs,

and their ten per cent

pay rise - asked Allah

so bemused?'

'I'll block their cynical

pay rise said God - it

really is absurd!'

We look down upon

the earth through our

magic lake,

But why must we hurt

innocent people - by

causing giant a giant

earthquake?'

'Surely it is better to resurrect a terrorist hero?
Call upon Sir Guy Fawkes - he'll go with the flow?'
'He can recruit some pals of his - and seize his magic moment,
Then make absolute certain - by dismissing the Houses of Parliament?'

'So, as both Good God and Allah stood up to plan their glory mission,
Good God wore his specs - as he wanted

twenty twenty vision!!!!

Allah said: 'Go on my

son - we will make

some changes'

And why won't you pay

me asked Allah - you

haven't paid me in

ages?'

'Shut up whinging, said

Good God to Allah, I

feed you as you know,'

'Yes, you do, said Allah -

but my last pay rise was

so low!'

'I told you, stop your

moaning - we need to

save the earth.

We need to stick together,

for a glorious new rebirth.'

So the intrepid duo went

on their quest - as the

sun set over yon,

And both Good God and

Allah - did an almighty

yawn!!!!

You, see, the world is

always on the edge - of

insanity, that people cause,

Don't forget my friends -

'Good God and Allah both

know: 'they both do rule

the shores!!!!'

BY DARRYL ASHTON

GOOD GOD AND ALLAH'S TASTY LAMB KEBAB

I love to get together

with Good God for

some tea,

We always enjoy a

kebab - as I get it

all for free!

I like to spread the

chili sauce all over

the tasty meat,

And wash it all down

with beer - a cool,

and delicious treat!

We chat about our

differences - and

we put the world to

right,

Then we drink some
more beer - we have
a real good night.
I have to use a napkin,
to keep my long
beard clean,
As anything can get
stuck in there - and
you can smell the
Mr Sheen!!!!

I'm always open to a
freebie - I cannot
deny that,
But I do object to
standing up - and doff
my stupid hat!!!!
We are talking about
merging - as one god

is not enough,

But when I mention

Allah - do I call his

bluff?

Two Gods are better

than one - that we

do discuss.

But sometimes on

occasions - we cause

a lot of fuss?

Kneeling down to have

a chat - but my knees

are now all knackered,

The pain it causes is

it real? My God! I feel

so shattered!!!!

We are now at peace -

that's for sure - as we

talk about the land,

But I am concerned as

I think it's wrong - when

God tries to hold my hand!!!!

That's you're lot - as I

am going - to work upon

my slab,

But thank you God for

giving me - a tasty lamb

kebab!!!!

BY DARRYL ASHTON

GOOD GOD AND ALLAH - ARE SERIOUSLY BOTH CONFUSED

Allah and Good God

were walking hand

in hand,

When they both

started singing -

and dancing to a

band.

The were wearing

pink shoulder bags -

and walking side by

side,

But all they really

wanted to do - was

go and permanently

hide!!

The felt so confused -

of how they both

did feel,

They weren't too

darn happy - they

didn't feel real!!!!

What is happening

to us - and why are

we wearing makeup?

Every time I wear it

I want to go and

throw up!!!!

We are as sad as

those humans - we

should not feel this

way -

What the heck is

happening - I do

feel such dismay?

We are both into

prayers - and we

should pray we do

get better,

We should not feel

like this - we feel

at the end of our

tether!!!!

We should now go

to the doctor - and

see what they

prescribe -

We want to be

normal again - not

like a blinking tribe!!

We do not like holding

hands - that is not

so right,

We look at Adam and
Eve - that is straight,
such delight.

We even read the
bible - but it doesn't
mention being queer?
Oh, my god, we both
do say; 'we really need
a beer!!!!'
"Who the heck is queer -
that is NOT what we
are?
It's just a malicious
rumour - we need to
call our pa!!!!

It really is is a funny
world that these

humans have all created,
They even marry same-
sex people - this really
should be deleted!!!!
Let's get together and
discuss what we should
do;
'We should bring normality
back - and condemn'
the PC crew!!!!'

We must now reflect on
this - and make amends
real quick,
And if those gay rights
object to us - we'll give
them a good swift kick!!
We will NOT tolerate
this unnatural behaviour,

Because this really wasn't

the intentions - of our true

God' the holy life creator!!!!

BY DARRYL ASHTON

GOOD GOD AND ALLAH GET DRUNK

Good God came home
and found he had no
dinner,
Then Allah said to Good
God; 'you really should
be thinner!!'
"I want my tasty kippers
and apple pie and cream,
Followed by cheese and
biscuits - I bet they taste
supreme!!"

Allah said; 'you eat too
much - you are so very
greedy,
And all this lovely food -
could be given to the

needy!!!!'

Oh, stop your moaning -

I am so very hungry,

And Allah put his apron

on - and pretended to

play mummy!!!!

They both sat down

and ate all their food,

Then after drinking lots

of whisky - they were

in a very drunken mood.

Shall we have a smoke -

a fine Cabana cigar?

Then we can sing some

songs - and play a nice

guitar!!

Why are we the sinners -

we act like the earthling'

humans?

And we cannot really

dance - I have such very

sore bunions!!!!

Let us drink to peace and

love - as we are two

great Gods;

'And just like those tasty

peas - we're from the

same old pod!!!!'

BY DARRYL ASHTON

TASTY KFC - IS A MEAL FIT FOR A KING

Tasty KFC is a favourite treat

of mine,

Especially when I eat it with

a glass of chilled white wine.

Or you can have a coke - that

is very good,

Just like KFC - that I know

it should.

Tasty chicken legs - or tasty

chicken breast -

Complete with lots of potato

fries - it simply is the best!

Finger licking' good - as you

constantly lick your lips,

Munching all that tasty chicken -

and those deep fried chips.

But if you eat too much of
it - you'll expand around the
waist,
But once you start to eat it -
you won't feel too much haste!
There are also side dishes -
like sweetcorn and chicken
sauce,
All adding to the calories -
naughty, but of course!!

So get down to your KFC -
and have a feast of a king,
Just lick your lips as you
know how - you've eaten
everything!!
You really can't deny it - for
you and also for me,

Bring on that tasty chicken -

in the form of KFC!!!!

BY DARRYL ASHTON

THE GAY RIGHTS CAUSE QUITE A SHAKE - OVER A GAY CREAM CAKE

I am a little fairy cake -

and my friend is called;

'cup',

We sit on the little shelf

all day long - preparing

our little prenup!

Our cream is light and

fluffy - and we love

the colour pink,

But lately some gay

rights group - has really

caused a stink!!

Now we are made by

a bakery - who have

a devout Christian belief,

And they are always

obliging - to make a

cake without any

grief.

But recently a vicious

group of gay rights -

set out to bully the

bakery,

And even took them all

to court - and used their

odious trickery!!

They bullied this bakery,

as they hated their

Christian stance,

And with the help of

legal aid - they led a

merry dance!

They saw the signs of

compensation - from

which they preached

their views,

And now from the

courts - the 'gay' cake

has made world news!!

This really is the icing -

on a "gay cake" for these

activists -

And all they ever wanted

to do - was show their

limp-wristed fists!!!

The judge showed no

mercy - and branded

the Christian bakery -

When the real people

who are at fault - grinned

at their cynical trickery!!

All this hassle over a

cake - and a 'fairy' one

of that,

Next time you see a cake -

just kindly doff your hat!!

The bakery in question -

I really wish them well,

And for the gay brigade

that brought the case;

'they can all go back to

their prison cell!!!!'

BY DARRYL ASHTON

WELCOME TO MEERKAT HOLLYWOOD MOVIES

"Look? Sergei? We're in the

Hollywood movies?"

"Oh, I see, Sergei sighs – as

he gently rubs his eyes."

They pinch a buggy and go

for a ride – around the film

set scenes,

While Sergei asks Aleksandr;

'have you been eating beans?'

Welcome to Hollywood movies, -

in good old America –

Sergei is driving the buggy – and

he's drinking a sarsparilla!

Oh, my god, Sergei, we have

to be professional –

We can't afford insurance –

for us to be in hospital!

They are driving into chaos —

as they both scream and

shout —

Sergei's driving like an idiot —

of that, there is no doubt!

Sergei is now panicking — and

misses his new computermabob,

But lately he's been over

eating — and turned into a

little slob!

With everyone chasing them,

they have caused a lot of

damage —

Aleksandr looks at Sergei -

and looks at all the carnage.

We are here to make a movie,

Sergei – not cause lots of mess,

Who will we crash into next –

it could be Elliott Ness!!

We are now the untouchables –

and we are from Meerkovo –

We are on our American mission

– and Sergei thinks he's Columbo!

Please, Sergei, drive with care –

we have to see the sights –

But everywhere were they go –

they're causing lots of fights!!

Then their buggy stops for a

while – and Aleksandr sighs –

Sergei is so bemused – he

very nearly cries.

"Sergei? Get a grip? And stop

playing with that pimple –

We have to conquer America –

we thought it would be simple!!

We should have brought Oleg –

but we left him in Africa –

He would have loved Hollywood –

in good old America!

So, ladies and gentlemen – we

say sit comfortables, please;

And both Sergei and Aleksandr

say; 'Welcome to Meerkat

Hollywood Movies.'

We now have to say goodbye,

to Arnold Schwarzenegger,

And go and collect baby Oleg –

in sunny Africa.

Please, continue to follow us –

in the Meerkat Hollywood

Movies –

We all have to be professional –

just like The Three Stooges!!!!

We will be back I promise you –

my word to you all, I give,

But Sergei is acting quite stupid –

he's turned into a spiv!!!!

We now head home to our

mansion house – and Sergei

plays with his pimple;

'The Meerkat Hollywood Movies

is born – it was so incredibly...

SIMPLE!!!!'

BY DARRYL ASHTON

WE ARE THE TSB BANKING DIRECTORS

We are the TSB bank -

we always like to say;

'yes!'

But on the other hand -

we like to cause you

stress!

People, ask us for a

loan - we can do this

if we want too,

But we only ever say

yes, to a select

privileged few!

Our directors have

now sold out - the

Spanish have flashed

their cash -

With all the money

we have made - we

will now have to dash!

Another UK bank is

bought by a foreign

source,

We ask ourselves

was this good for us -

we all replied; of

course!'

Nothing now is British -

oh, what a shame!

But we have all made

a killing - it is the name

of the game!

Yes, we'll inform our

customers - but when

the time is right,

We don't really care

anymore - as money

is so tight!

The Spanish now are

in charge - I'm sure

they'll all speak English -

But if they are all

automated - I bet they

all speak gibberish!

We were the bank that

really cared - as we've

made a lot of money -

So our message to all

you customers: 'we

were so very phony!'

So now we say goodbye

to you - as we head

off to pastures new,

Clutching our fat

bonuses - we're rich

because of you!

Thank you to the

Spanish - they paid

over the odds,

But if the truth be

really known - we

bankers are greedy

sods!!

BY DARRYL ASHTON

THE ENVIRONMENT TOSSERS

Who are the 'tossers' who
simply don't care,
Tossing it here and tossing
it there?
A swarm of litter bugs, out
on control,
On the run or just out for
a stroll?

A coffee to go, a box from
KFC,
Into the bin, where it's
meant to be!
It drifts along the pavement,
it drifts across the road,
Knee-deep in rubbish, not

paved with gold!

Landfills overflowing, with
double-wrapped debris,
From the humble crisp bag
to a rubbishy old settee!
A throw-away society, we
throw away a lot,
Our lazy population, who
couldn't give a jot!

Fly tipping is the norm,
they wait 'til after dark,
Bring back the rag-and-
bone man, with his horse
and cart.
Scooping up the droppings,
the perfect veggie feed,
The ultimate recycling, to

germinate your seed!

Cutting down a tree, it
makes us want to weep,
Just to make the litter
that's blowing down the
street!
It stood there for many
years, helping us to
breath,
A newspaper in the end,
just for us to read.

Spare a thought for the
tree, with its leafy crown,
Next time you hold a
paper, about to throw it
down.
Exploited by man, it didn't

deserve its fate,

To make all the litter, that

conjures up such hate!

BY DARRYL ASHTON

TWINKLETOES

I've seen a little fairy - she

is so warm and bright -

And when we have a chat -

she really is a delight.

She tells me of a magic

land - which is so far away,

She then invites me to go

there - as I do shout; 'Hip-pip

HOORAY!'

The fairy's name is

Twinkletoes - she really

is so cute,

And every time I see her -

she's always eating fruit!

I marvel at her little figure -

which is so very tiny,

And would you believe it -

she loves to wear a bikini!

She is so very friendly -

and she is so very

beautiful,

But she's always being

hassled by an evil little

troll.

She loves to wear a silver

dress, and shiny pretty

shoes,

And when the darkness

falls - she loves to sing

the blues.

She also loves to dance

away - and drink a little

soda -

Then when a handsome

prince dances with her -

he kisses her little shoulder.

They glide across the

shiny dance floor - they

are the stars of the floor,

When suddenly the music

stops - everyone shouts;

'MORE!'

Her beautiful name is

Twinkletoes - but she's

only visible to me -

She's lives in my

imagination - she's always

very happy.

But she does have many

friends - and a few who

want to hurt her,

But her handsome prince

charming - loves to caress

her hair.

We don't know much about

her - we'll have to ask

her creator -

Darryl Ashton is the only

one - he really does know

her.

She came from a surreal

mind - and a lot of

imagination -

Now when she does appear -

she causes a sensation.

So if we close our eyes a

while - and make a little

wish;

'Perhaps we'll see Twinkletoes -

looking really swish?'

But for now she's back

home in bed - as she strokes

her tiny nose,

Will she reappear again? Darryl

Ashton...is the only one who

knows!

BY DARRYL ASHTON

ASDA MEETS GEORGE

"Hello George, how are you?

Oh, I'm good thank you, how

do you do!

My name is ASDA – and I love

your clothes –

Especially the ones you call;

ya' "drawers!"

I see you hanging about on

those hooks,

I see all them' knickers – and

those sexy little bloomers!

All different colours are there

to be seen,

Oh, please let me look – I'm so

terribly keen!

Walking around admiring those
sales girls,
Can I be cheeky – and ask for a
twirl?
The girls are all charming – that
is so true,
But when I walk away – there's a
big queue!

So get down to ASDA, and you will
see George –
All those garments – some can be
yours.
Black silk, and French knickers – It's
all on display;
"Go their today – It'll make your day!"

The tiller-girls are all cute – they're
just passed the fruit,

I said: "I like your knickers – they are really cute!"

I get through the checkout – and I say goodbye;

"Thank you, to George, you really caught my eye!"

BY DARRYL ASHTON

ASDA'S POTATO CRISPS

Well, what a delight, it has to be said,
Don't buy Walker's crisps – buy ASDA's' instead!
Full of flavour – and very tasty too,
But you'll have to be quick – and join the queue!

I saw these crisps while in their store –
I couldn't believe it – bargains galore!
From chocolate bars to cakes and bread,
Fresh fish too – and a cafe to tread.

But those crisps are all great – I

kid you not,

While I fight with my bags – they're

all in a knot!

But it's those crisps I've discovered,

oh what a treat,

But now I'm tired – dead on my feet!

You can shake the bag – and

wake the crisps,

While you trot to the checkout –

licking your lips!

Oh, those bargains, I kid you

not,

I've dropped my phone – oh I'm

a clot!

A friend of mine is a charming

soul,

Callum's the name – listening

for the call!

A team leader he is – and always

so friendly,

When he does see me – he calls me;

"Sergie!"

Then there's a beauty, a lady so

cute, the Lady Dawn – oh she's

a darling.

I go there often and hope to see –

the lady Dawn, especially in the

morning!

To see the staff as they are all

friendly,

So get down to ASDA – it is you're

destiny.

But those crisps are great - I kid

you not,

Go and try them – off you all trot!

Tell the manager - they are all nicer,

Happy shopping my friends,

compliments of ASDA!

BY DARRYL ASHTON

ONWARD CHRISTIAN POETS

(To the tune of; Onward Christian Soldiers)

(It may help if you do sing along!)

Onward Christian poets,
its time to call our bluff,
You can write with harmony –
because you know your stuff.
Write the rhyme my poet friends,
Then you'll start new trends,
Onward to annoy the folk,
and write some more sick jokes!

(Chorus)

Onward Christian poets – writing as they go,
Waving to the crowd they do – with Christmas time in tow!

Onward then ye poets,
Christmas is now here,
See those decorations – why do we not cheer?
See those festive Christmas trees – and those fairy lights,
Dazzling on the festive branch, a monstrous sight delights!

(Chorus)

Onward Christian poets,

moaning at the sights,

They are not that happy -

they've lost their human

rights!

Onward then ye poets,

sing as you do write,

Writing all those poems,

it is your human right.

People will complain to

you, but you ignore

them, true,

All they do is whinge

and moan – oh I need

the loo!

(Chorus)

Onward Christian poets,

we suffer writer's cramp,

Now my failing eyesight,

where's my bleeding'

lamp?!

Onward Christian poets,

battling PC crap,

But when they read their

poems – we give them all

a clap!

Writing poems of MPs,

and about their sleaze,

Brussels spout their

dictating views – their

expenses we will freeze!

(Chorus)

Onward Christian poets,

smiling as they type,

But sometimes they will

admit – they write a load

of tripe!

Onward Christian poets,

feeling quite depressed,

All they want for Christmas,

is something very blessed.

Listening to the garbage –

that's on the TV news,

So we'll write a whole lot

more – and then we'll have

a snooze!

(Chorus)

Onward Christian poets,

running out of ink,

All that poetry writing,

sure does make us think!

Onward Christian poets,

off to church we go,

Singing all those Christmas

hymns, 'oh diddly oh!'

Oh we need a drink or two,

but we may get drunk –

Give me now my sparkling

hooch – then we'll write

more junk!

(Chorus)

Onward Christian poets,

we wish you all the best,

Not many can write poetry,

so we'll put you to the test!

Onward Christian poets,

writing in the States,

They are all together –

eating juicy steaks.

Lots of pampered poets –

eating to their fill.

Now they're full from

over-eating – now they

need a pill!

(Chorus)

Onward Christian poets,

touring in the States,

But they keep on writing -

about their own mistakes.

Finally ye poets – they all

gather round –

Writing about Good God –

now they're heaven bound.

Onward now and forward –

they love their writing fate,

All aboard the poet train –

and it's bleeding' late!

(Chorus)

Onward Christian poets,

you we all adore,

So let's all celebrate poems –

we all want some more!

BY DARRYL ASHTON

THE TRIBES OF BONGO BONGO LAND - PART TWO

The tunes of Bongo Bongo land – are played by the band,
But all the seats are taken – and people now do stand.

The Bongo Bongo drums beat out – as the natives call their witch doctor,
But who does have the magic potion – that can really cure?

I see the tribe all dancing – around the tribal fire,
Also indulging, in whatever they do desire!

The tribe is now invaded –
by Cameron and Obama –
But they are themselves
caught – as they try to
steal a banana!

We must send out a clear
message – to all those
world police,
That if any world leaders
who invade our space –
will end up as grated
cheese!

We must inform you all –
that UK MPs taste sour,
Even when on a skewer –
and we rub cover their

heads in flour!

Obama and David
Cameron, they are all
on the menu,
Their heads will be
shrunk – this I promise
you!

Obama is on the fire –
and his balls are fiercely
burning –
While Cameron is next
in line – his stomach is
now churning.

"Oh my god, shouts Obama,
we're on the bloody menu!"
"Take it like a man, mutters

Cameron – now I've lost my shoe!"

"Sod your shoes, wails Obama,
as he's slowly being roasted,"
Where the heck is Steven
Seagal – when he's really
wanted?"

What about the Expendables?
they could come and help us?
That is pure Hollywood – it is
a lot of fuss!

It's okay for you to be calm –
and not give a toss,
Wait till you are being roasted –
I'll drink to your sad loss!

Why did we come here – to

meet these friendly folk?

We didn't come invited – we

invaded through the smoke!

The natives of Bongo Bongo –

freed them as a pardon

Now go back home – and

don't you dare – return

with George Osborne!

So, off they both went –

away from the Bongo Bongo –

Until the next chapter my

dears – I'm off for a game

of BINGO!!

Both Cameron and Obama –

have learnt their lesson well,

The next time you invade

somewhere – be careful who

you tell!!

BY DARRYL ASHTON

THE TRIBES OF BONGO BONGO LAND

The tunes of Bongo Bongo
land - are played by the
band,
But all the seats are taken -
and people now do stand.
The Bongo Bongo drums
beat out - as the natives
call their witch doctor,
But who does have the
magic potion - that can
really cure?

I see the tribe all dancing -
around the tribal fire,
Also indulging, in whatever
they do desire!
The tribe is now invaded -

by Cameron and Obama -

But they are themselves

caught - as they try to

steal a banana!

We must send out a clear

message - to all those world

police,

That if any world leaders who

invade our space - will end

up as grated cheese!

We must inform you all - that

UK MP's taste sour,

Even when on a skewer -

they're always on the scour!

Obama and David Cameron,

they are all on the menu,

Their heads will be shrunk -

this I promise you!

Then we shall dance away -

until a new tomorrow -

Courtesy of our tribal gang -

in the tribal' Bongo Bongo!!!!

BY DARRYL ASHTON

THE HOMELESS

The homeless are not
aliens - they are human,
just like us all,
Its just they've had
some bad luck - and
on hard times they
do fall.

They scour the streets
of the land,
Hoping a kind stranger
will give them a helping
hand,
They lay in the cold of
winter - inside their
cardboard box,
And if they catch a chill -

they might catch chicken

pox!

We see this problem

every day - and it really

shouldn't happen,

When mankind fails to

act - loneliness will ripen.

To be cast aside like a doll,

and to be jeered at every

day,

When all the homeless

really want - is to feel

a-okay!

This is a serious problem -

and especially now,

We must find a way to

stop this - provide some

shelter, somehow.

Roaming the streets isn't

the answer - and not in

this day and age,

And when the local

authorities ignore it - it

puts me in a rage!

We could provide more

centres - and food and

drink to share,

And a friendly chatter -

before this is so rare?

Just to listen - and to

smile - this could prove

a lifesaver,

Then if you can afford it -

donate a nice new dollar!

This happens all over -
even in poor countries
too,
It is poverty - and children
suffer, I tell you this is
true.
People in high places who
live in posh big houses,
They don't know the real
truth - they can't see past
their own noses!

Welfare is partly to blame -
with the poor losing their
welfare
If they are disabled - they'll
lose all - and that's not
fair.
They target the disabled -

and the vulnerable of society,

It isn't right, I tell you - they

need help - and on occasions

pity?

Food banks are now popular

all over the land we see,

They provide food and advice -

for you and for me.

The rich just get richer - and

the poor are left to rot,

And as the single mother - lays

her baby in a broken cot.

The world would be a better

place - if poverty wasn't here,

But there's nothing we can

do about it - but try to bring

good cheer.

A simple smile, a simple wave,
this really would be better,
And if more people spoke to
each other - things would
improve forever.

But this is not an ideal world -
and there are a lot of sinners,
But they can be reformed - and
be the new beginners!
The homeless could be a thing
of the past - and this I so do
pray;
"Especially at times like this -
some warmth on Christmas Day."

So, please, spare a thought -
and if you can a smile,
And watch the face light up -

instead of going on trial!

This is my prediction - to end

all poverty -

But I can't do it alone - I need

help, seriously!

From government leaders -

to council sinners - their help

is what we need,

And maybe one fine day – we

will all say; 'they did a very

good deed.'

So embrace your life as never

before - and say; 'thank you

for your warm home,'

Because if you weren't so

lucky - the streets you may

just roam?

BY DARRYL ASHTON

THE HOMELESS - PART TWO

The homeless do need
help - not condemnation
every day,
We should help them
more - in our own way.
A smile and a chat - or
a cup of tea to give,
And maybe a sandwich -
we all should forgive.

It happens every day -
and they feel such
dismay,
The homeless are all
human - this is true
today?
Walking the streets

they do - often feeling

low,

But we can make a

little difference - and

good cheer is good to

know.

The homeless just

want a home - just like

you and me;

'They're even willing to

pay for it - in rent for

all to see?'

The bedroom tax doesn't

help them - nor the local

authorities;

If they help the homeless

to get a home - they're

hit by a sanctions swizz!!

The homeless want to

work - and pay taxes like

all other people -

They don't want any hand-

outs - this is pure and

simple.

The welfare advisers

are like computers -

"Next person, please? It's

all electronic disorders?"

The homeless wander

from place to place -

Just trying to get a grip

on the human race?

In cold weather they

will freeze -

In warm weather - they

feel at ease!

But, being homeless isn't

nice - and no one should

live like this -

If only with a little help -

their life could be so bliss!

A hot bath - and a good

hot meal, can perk your

spirits high,

And when you're out of

the rain - your clothes will

feel so dry?

A little compassion - and

a will to care -

To eradicate this homeless

problem - we do it because

we dare?

We can all help solve this

problem - that is so very
true -
If you see a homeless
person - say; 'hello, - how
are you?'
Give a little blessing - and
see their face light up with
glee,
And you will see with your
own eyes - being friendly is
so FREE!

So my new year message
to the government, is to try
to help the poor -
Give them all some hope -
don't rob their benefits
even more?
Make 2015 a happy year -

and try and spread good

cheer,

But just from me - and the

lord - I wish you all; A

Happy New Year.

BY DARRYL ASHTON

WE ARE THE REFUGEES

I am a refugee and I

do feel so very weak,

When we enter another

country - they just

turn the other cheek.

We are fleeing from

persecution - and we

seek a new land home,

But we are so very

tired - as all we do is

roam.

We don't want much,

I swear to you - just

a new life and freedom.

Somewhere we can

call our home - and

look after our poorly
mum?
We've travelled from
the Syria - which isn't
very nice,
They really do harm us -
not just once, but twice.

We don't have many
possessions - just what
we all can carry -
We walk and we walk -
for many miles - feeling
very weary.
We were badly treated
by Hungary police,
But we had to fight and
continue - we have to
sacrifice.

Some have also perished -

in the water's to our new

land -

Seeing children's body's,

laying on the sand.

our sanctuary is our life -

and we know you will help

us,

That's why some nice people -

supplied us with a bus!

We really are so poor -

but we are also willing to

work,

We are all very friendly

people - and work, we do not

shirk.

Love and understanding - is

what the lord commands -
He has guided us all - to our
new and promised lands.

Children have also perished -
as so has mum and dad,
But we are still pursuing our
freedom - I bet you think
we're mad?
Many country's are helping
us - and we are very grateful,
All we want is food and water -
and to say a prayer, which is
plentiful.

People are so very kind - our
tears we all do shed,
Our children are so very tired -
they now sleep on a makeshift

bed.

Everyone is helping us - but we've had our share of heartache,
Watching loved ones drown at sea - it makes our hearts all break.

We lay down for the night to sleep and we gaze up at the starry skies,
Have we finally found a home - it really is a surprise.
We pray to God, our saviour - he helps us to find our grace,
And we can say a big thank you - to the European' human race.

BY DARRYL ASHTON

THE REFUGEES OF GOD-A HELPING HAND OF GOD

Lord God Almighty

came to earth, to

help the refugees,

He was very touched

by the images - so

he set out on a cloud

with ease.

His mission was to

help them - to find

them a place to live,

And try to reassure

them all - time will

always forgive.

He went to their aid,

and his angels did

go along,

Always by the lord's
side - always singing
a song.

They would help all
the refugees to find
their sanctuary -
And make their new
land a home - and
never more to worry.
The people were so
tired - and feeling
ever more desperate,
But they knew they
had to carry on - as
their promised land
was separate.

God smiled down on

them and he had to

help because;

'And promptly sent

them a gift - in the

form of a bus!'

Their relief was oh

so visible - they were

at breaking point,

They climbed aboard

these buses - to

Germany is to appoint.

This mammoth trek

across the land - to

find their sanctuary.

All of them prodding

on - as they try not

to worry.

They met some friendly

people - who offered
them food and water,
They really were so very
grateful - a thank you
they did whisper.

They all hold hands
together and hope to
reach their nation,
And God will have the
last say; 'if they find
their new destination?'
Huddled together - and
not knowing the
language - but they are
getting there,
The whole of Europe is
now helping - because
they really care.

They are human beings -
I see tears in their eyes,
But they are almost to
their rest - they tend to
look surprised!
God has intervened - as
only he can do -
He provides food and
water - but there is a
very long queue.

Their mammoth journey
is almost complete -
they've found their
Germany.
But we are inviting them -
to come to the UK.
It really is our nature -
to offer a helping hand,

And welcome these new

people - to our little Christian

land.

From tears, we have some

laughter - happiness is

now born.

To see the smiles upon

their faces - a new life

is now reborn.

Our God in heaven came

to help - to save his children's

lives,

And in doing this he lit the

light - to shine god's love

survives.

BY DARRYL ASHTON

BEATING MY DEPRESSION

I sit here and I wish away,

At the same time – I feel

dismay,

No feeling I have - and no

emotion I show,

The clock ticks away – and

it is painfully slow.

The world goes on – I see

that so clearly,

I used to love life – I mean

that so dearly.

Now it doesn't matter as it

isn't the same –

A horrible illness - makes me

feel insane.

I try to fight this illness, I've
unfortunately got,
It wrecks my brain – to total
rot.
The life is sucked from out
of my soul,
I daren't go out – in case I
feel small.

I try to look smart – that is
the key,
But no one can see my
enemy in me?
I always get compliments –
that is good –
But why does this not
improve my inner-self mood?

The whole world around me

seems to close in –

And I consider having a gin!

But this will not make me

feel any better –

The inner person inside me -

it just takes shelter.

People will stare – and people

will think –

They'll also judge you – before

you can blink!

What the heck – you must stay

calm,

You may need a friend – to hold

on to your arm?

Guidance, and tolerance – is the

name of the game,

So why aren't we treated just

the same?

Someone to listen — and someone to care,

Before I crack up — and jump through the air!

What makes me so sad? What has gone wrong?

Why do I hear a horrible gong?

To be free of this menace — and suffer no more,

Just to be happy — is what I adore.

Just to be free from this horrible illness —

And then to find happiness — and maybe forgiveness?

Where do I go? Where do I search?

Is the answer, my, friends,

somewhere in church?

In God's holy house – that's were I'll look,
Under the seats – but I feel like a crook!
Tablets I take – they help me to cope –
What are my options – to hang by a rope?

What is the cause? Is there any pause?
I want to get dressed – in my best clothes?
People still laugh – but I do not care –
I now feel good – and so does my hair.

This illness, I'm winning, and take each day as it comes,

I now feel better – no more aching bones!

Life has new meaning – I have a new mission –

This illness I had – it is known as;

DEPRESSION!!!!

BY DARRYL ASHTON

BEATING DEPRESSION

Sitting here in my chair

I just gaze outside – and

just stare.

I watch the world go

silently by,

I'd like to be there – as

I do cry.

My torment is in my soul,

and it is spreading,

I have to be punished –

but is this my ending?

I refuse to be beaten –

and I will fight my cause,

Because somewhere in

the future – I will fight,

I knows?

The tablets do help me –
they calm me down –
If I don't take them – my
brain would drown!
I look into the light – as
my soul feels so right –
This has to be the way –
the light is so bright?

No one can see how I
feel inside –
That's why most days
I do try to hide.
My inner self is what
I do feel,
I just want to get better –
and feel so real?

This hidden illness is not

so visible,

So people condemn you —

and it makes you feel ill.

They are so judgemental —

and also offensive -

They seem to look through

you — and see the negative?

Dear Lord, above, please

hear me now;

'Help me get through this —

I need hope, somehow?'

I know I can beat this

feeling, I suffer,

To be set free — while my

life takes a stutter.

I know with help I can

combat this illness —

All I feel is sadness – I

do feel a mess.

Please show me the way –

there must be a reason:

"Help me to beat my

horrible depression?"

I'm in your hands, I now

accept ,

I have sleepless nights –

I haven't yet slept.

To wake from my dream,

and feel so free,

To beat this depression –

I do ask of thee?

To summon the life that

was born unto me,

To hold your hand – and

smile with glee.

To go to places without
any fear,

Depression, be gone – I
so want to cheer?

I look at the sun in the
clear blue sky –
Oh, my goodness – I so
want to fly.
The world looks different –
and feels a pleasure,
No more depression – it
has gone forever.

You see, this dreadful
illness you cannot see,
But I'm not a monster –
I live by the sea.

To walk on air – and sing

out loud,

I beat depression – now

I love the crowd.

I say this to you – who may

suffer like me;

'Never give up – and you

will be free.'

Just pray to God as your now

in remission –

And, trust in God – as you

beat your depression.

BY DARRYL ASHTON

THE BRILLIANT SALVATION ARMY

The Salvation Army

are the true heroes,

They provide food

and shelter - and

also warm clothes.

They are a sanctuary -

as people do attend,

They are the

homeless people -

often at their wits

end.

A friendly chat, a

friendly ear, is what

they all do offer,

The Salvation Army

is a treat - to all

who's suffer's

tomorrow.

A sanctuary of a

safe place - and a

warm drink to warm

you through,

Everyone is welcome -

but, there may just

be a queue.

Come with me - and

take my hand -

We can sit and chat -

and listen to the brass

band?

Don't be sad - I'm

you're friend -

Together we can talk -

my coat you can lend!

The snow is falling

outside I see,

But we're inside - and

drinking some tea.

No one is lonely - as

we all do care,

No one should just

sit there - and sadly

stare.

We are the helpers

of the Salvation Army,

Because we do care -

just like your mummy.

The pipes of peace -

I hear them play,

The brilliant Salvation

Army says: 'Happy

Christmas Day.'

Twenty sixteen is a whole new year,
Let's take a drink - and spread good cheer?
No one should be lonely - and love will arrive,
Just hold out your hand - and people will survive.
Hail! Hail! The trend of the barmy -
All are helped by the brilliant;
'Salvation Army.'

Christmas time is here - and wars are

silent,

All this and more -

as the peace is

defiant.

We salute those

heroes who help

the poor,

Offer them sanctuary -

and a whole lot more.

God bless us all -

and also the sinners;

'The fabulous Salvation

Army - now serves -

Christmas Day Dinners.'

BY DARRYL ASHTON

THE STREETS I DID CALL HOME

I sit here in the

gutter - thinking

of my life,

One day I was

single - then one

day I had a wife.

Those days seem

a memory - and

so far away.

Now I'm in the

gutter - and all I

do is pray.

I sit here for no

good reason - well,

that is what I say;

'Every day is the

same - I have to
feel okay!'
People just walk
past me - and
they never ever
glance,
They're gazing in
to their phones -
like they're in a
trance!

I try to live each
day, as I see it
from my own
view,
But I did once
live a life - yes,
it was just like
you!

The days are

long - and

sometimes cold,

I wish I had a

loved one - to

cuddle and to

hold.

I wander round

the land of hope,

I see nothing in

the future;

'I always pray to

God up high - a

life he might just

nurture?'

I wear my dirty

and scruffy rags -

I once was very

smart,

But one bad day

I found the devil -

my life just fell

apart.

All I want is a

friend - but every

one's too busy.

I'd love to live in

the countryside -

boy, do I hate the

city!

I will, again, pray

to God - and hope

he hears my

prayer,

Then he can tell

me once and for

all; 'If he really
does care!'

Christmas Day is
the same as every
other day.
But on occasions
people ask me:
'Darryl, are you a-
okay?'
'Yes, I am, I just
roam the streets -
and quote my
poetry -
'Because no matter
where I go in life -
my writing's are
there for me.

But one fine day I

wrote a poem -

about our lord and

master.

I then saw a light

so bright - it was

so very sinister.

The light guided

me to a pathway

to a new found

home -

So from this day

on - my new life

does start - away

from the streets I

used to roam.

BY DARRYL ASHTON

THOSE GAY RIGHTS ACTIVISTS

Now gay marriage is legal,

we can cause so much

affray,

We'll target those Christians -

and cause mass dismay.

We have got the green

light - to cause so much

trouble,

But when we go to court -

money is so adorable!!

The Christians can't object,

to 'same-sex' marriage now,

And should they dare try -

in court their heads will

bow.

Our 'same-sex' marriage is

equal - but not in God's

holy lands,

He doesn't like it when he

sees gay couples "proudly"

holding hands.

But when they get on their

band wagon - and start to

preach their views,

They really make me sick -

they really don't amuse.

Marriage is for a couple,

a man and a woman,

Not two men or two women,

it has to be spoken.

The green light shines so

bright upon the vicious

views,

When all the poison will

come from - the 'gay mouths',

in the loos.

So, my message to this

gay brigade, is stop spreading

your vicious crews!!!!

We all know you ponder at;

'always making the news'.

BY DARRYL ASHTON

ABBOTT AND COSTELLO IN - THE SUPER DUPER COMPUTER STORE

Bud Abbott is now a shop owner and runs a thriving business that sells computers. Lou Costello rings Bud to hopefully buy a computer – and this is the conversation that follows…

Costello calls to buy a computer from Abbott…

ABBOTT: Super Duper computer store. Can I help you?

COSTELLO: Thanks, I'm setting up an office in my den and I'm thinking about buying a computer?

ABBOTT: Mac?

COSTELLO: No, the name's Lou.

ABBOTT: Your computer.

COSTELLO: I don't own a computer. I want to buy one.

ABBOTT: Mac?

COSTELLO: I told you, my name's Lou.

ABBOTT: What about Windows?

COSTELLO: Why? Will it get stuffy in here?

ABBOTT: Do you want a computer with Windows?

COSTELLO: I don't know. What will I see when I look at the windows?

ABBOTT: Wallpaper.

COSTELLO: Never mind the windows. I need a computer and software.

ABBOTT: Software for Windows?

COSTELLO: No, on the computer! I need something I can use to write proposals, track expenses and run my business. What do you have?

ABBOTT: Office.

COSTELLO: Yeah, for my office. Can you recommend anything?

ABBOTT: I just did.

COSTELLO: You just did what?

ABBOTT: Recommend something.

COSTELLO: You recommended something?

ABBOTT: Yes.

COSTELLO: For my office?

ABBOTT: Yes.

COSTELLO: OK, what did you recommend for my office?

ABBOTT: Office.

COSTELLO: Yes, for my office!

ABBOTT: I recommend Office with Windows.

COSTELLO: I already have an office with windows! OK, let's just say I'm sitting at my computer and I want to type a proposal. What do I need?

ABBOTT: Word.

COSTELLO: What word?

ABBOTT: Word in Office.

COSTELLO: The only word in office is office.

ABBOTT: The Word in Office for Windows.

COSTELLO: Which word in office for Windows?

ABBOTT: The Word you get when you click the blue 'W'.

COSTELLO: I'm going to click your blue 'W' if you don't start coming up with some straight answers! What about book – keeping? Do you have anything to track my money?

ABBOTT: Money.

COSTELLO: That's right. What do you have?

ABBOTT: Money.

COSTELLO: I need money to track my money?

ABBOTT: It comes bundled with your computer.

COSTELLO: What's bundled with my computer?

ABBOTT: Money.

COSTELLO: Money comes with my computer?

ABBOTT: Yes. At no extra charge.

COSTELLO: I get a bundle of money with my computer? How much?

ABBOTT: One copy.

COSTELLO: Isn't it illegal to copy money?

ABBOTT: Microsoft gave us a licence to copy Money.

COSTELLO: They can give you a licence to copy money?

ABBOTT: Why not? They own it!

(A few days later…)

ABBOTT: Super Duper computer store. Can I help you?

COSTELLO: How do I turn my computer off?

ABBOTT: Click on 'Start'.

THE END

Produced and Written

BY DARRYL ASHTON

THERE IS A GREEN HILL FAR AWAY – REVISED

There is a green hill far away

outside the city wall,

Where the drunks all go and

drink their stuff and then they

try to crawl.

There is a green hill far away

upon the mountain top -

The gypsies gather in their

crowds and empty all their

slop!

There is a green hill down

the road at the traffic lights,

Where all the cars go

speeding through - especially

on dark nights.

There is a green hill up for sale
and money always talks,
So when a supermarket opens
up - the prices always chokes!

God help us now we are all
doomed, as the heatwave is now
here,
So get me to the dirty pub and
I'll drink a nice cold beer!

So, there was once a very green
hill looking oh so grand,
But the builders came and waved
their cash - and promptly bought
the land.

Fear not you MPs you are all
doomed, and Guy Fawkes is now

here,

At last his mission is now complete

and we all drink and cheer!

There was a green hill in the town

where people used their phones,

But now they are all stuck up there

and looking just like clones!

Thank you oh Allah and Good God

too, I see you on the hill,

What's this I hear of Cherie Blair -

she gives the crowds a thrill!

I say farewell to this green hill as

the phone masts do invade,

If I catch you phoning home you

lot - I'll hit you with my spade.

Thank god he's saved the holy

life and Allah sings the blues,

But now he sings the white man's

blues and promptly blew a fuse!

THE END

BY DARRYL ASHTON

THERE IS A GREEN HILL FAR AWAY - PART TWO

There is a green hill far

away without any sign

of life,

Where a man can go

and enjoy himself and

escape his nagging wife!

There is a green hill far

away were women go

to rest,

Escaping from their house-

wife image – and now

they flee the nest.

There is a green hill in

a prison were Rolf Harris

was sent to paint,

He's now in moping in a

cell and duly he feels faint.

There is a green hill in

the town were Stonewall

go to praise,

If they can't have their

gay cream cake their

eye brows they will raise!

There is a green hill up

the road were a Mosque

stands so proud,

But when you enter and

praise the Allah – you'll

join the converted crowd!

There was a green hill so

far away were asylum is

a trade,

But if they earn more than you – you hit them with a spade!

There is a green hill in the street were people all do meet,

They congregate and cause mayhem – they think it's all a treat!

There is a green hill so far away were Allah and God, do meet,

They sit on down and have a drink – God says; "You have big feet!"

There is a green hill so far away were Christians were harassed,
The gay rights asked for a nice 'gay cake' and shouted human rights!

Oh god there is a nice green hill so very far away,
Were Stonewall should be banished too – and we all do shout; "HOORAY!"

BY DARRYL ASHTON

AN ALIEN REBIRTH FOR PLANET EARTH

There came a knock on my front door,
And there stood an alien 12 foot four,
With waving tentacles and skin of green,
Not the prettiest sight I'd ever seen.

'Sorry to trouble you,' one head said,
'But my spaceship's battery is quite dead.
'I come in peace, so have no fear,
'From a place that's cosmically quite near.'

'Sure, help yourself,' I
couldn't be rude,
'Can I get you a coffee or
perhaps some food?'
'That's awfully kind,'
another head said,
'My name translates to
the Earth name Fred.'

We pottered about and
got his battery fixed,
He spoke of his journey
and the awful risks
Of interstellar flight and
how warping space
Can get you quickly from
place to place.

He spoke of his planet and

its binary suns,

And how quaint it is

we've got just one,

So I asked if he'd take me

for a ride

And he said: 'No probs,

just step inside.'

In the blink of an eye, we

arrived on Gluck

And I climbed outside to

take a look,

Two blazing suns in

cloudless skies

Shone so bright it hurt

my eyes.

Fred showed me around

and I have to say

I can't remember when

I'd had such a day,

Breathtaking wonders and

awesome sights

And time slipped by at

the speed of light.

I saw seas of red and

trees of blue

Flora and fauna of every

hue.

All that I saw overflowed

with life

No hint of pain or hate or

strife.

In time I suddenly turned

to Fred:

'Can you take me home?

It's time for bed.'

But I saw Fred's eyes all

fill with tears,

And he said: 'It just

confirmed our fears.

'You humans don't deserve

the Earth,

'You've no idea just what

it's worth.

'You poison the land and

poison the seas,

'You poison the lakes and

butcher the trees.

'You poison the air and

animals die,

'I saw all these things

and it made me cry.

'I'll take you back to your

dying Earth,

'That globe that gave you

species birth.

'You're time is over, as

we take over,

'We'll look after the Earth,

we'll live in clover.

'But you were kind to me,

I call you friend,

'I'll come back for you just

before the end.'

BY DARRYL ASHTON

JUST TO CARE

Oh Lord, let the world
be a better place,
With love between
nations, regardless of
race.
Let the fighting stop
and the loving begin.
To care for your
neighbour is such a
kind thing.

So many people need
help these days,
We can be of service
in so many ways.
Old Mr Bilby, who's in
some pain,

Is waiting to have his

hip done again.

I get his prescriptions

and food for the week,

And buy him a cream

cake, just for a treat.

Mrs Tate's bunions

have just been done,

I'll pop in and see her,

I promised her son.

Frail Mrs Carey loves

a ride in my car,

Providing that we don't

travel too far.

She sits up straight so

she can be seen,

And, waving her hand,

pretends she's the Queen.

Miss Moon waits for me
in her wheelchair,
We will go to the park;
she loves the fresh air.
I guess a knock on the
door and a cheery smile
Makes the old folks happy,
at least for a while.

On Friday I'll look after
young Sarah Jane,
While her mother goes
for a scan once again.
There are always dear
friends who live far
away,
So I write lots of letters

to brighten their day.

My day is complete,

after helping these folk,

They really do love – a

jolly good talk.

My job is rewarding, I

love so much,

The old folk are friendly,

friendships we touch.

To care and to be friendly,

is my only reward,

I do not wish anyone to be

on a ward.

My work is hard, but it is

so healthy,

Especially when my smile,

makes the old folk so happy.

As I climb into my bed I give a big sigh,

I'm tired, but happy – can you guess why?

Tomorrow is a new day, and blessed in its own way,

When those old folk do see me – they'll all shout...

hooray!

BY DARRYL ASHTON

MY CARER

You care for me because you care,

But all I do is sit and stare.

You give me friendship and a smile,

And all I do is run a mile.

You are always there, no matter what,

You are so punctual – in your time slot.

I can't bathe myself – you are there,

I feel ashamed -- but you do care.

Feelings are there – but I still care,

You never grumble – you're always there.

I moan and moan – but you still smile,

I expect you soon – to run a mile!

I thank god you are there, as I am

alone,

I live alone in my home sweet home.

You are my treasure – and I do care,

You are my carer – you are always

there.

BY DARRYL ASHTON

CHRISTMAS MORNING - WITH ALF GARNETT JNR

The misery guts on Christmas Morning!

Christmas Morning...With Alf Garnett jnr!

(This is based on both the classic US and UK TV sitcoms of All In The Family, which starred Archie Bunker - and the Til Death Us Do Part - starring Warren Mitchell as the bigoted and loud mouth Alf Garnett - which actually did inspire . All In The Family.)

(Some strong language is included in this feature)

(Alf wakes up with a hangover)

ALF: "Oh, my head!"

ELSIE: "Serves you right! Stopping out till all hours, drinking and smoking.

Now you're fit for nothing!"

ALF: "Shaddap, you silly moo!"

ELSIE: "Do you want some breakfast?"

ALF: "No, I bloody don't! Just a cup of tea!"

ELSIE: "I don't know what I'm gonna do with this!"

ALF: "With what?"

ELSIE: "This, turkey, you bought from the market! It's too big!"

ALF: "Just cook it...and we'll all bloody well eat it!"

ELSIE: "A nice bit of pork would have done us! This will be wasted!"

ALF: "Oh, stop yer nagging, will you! Just bloody well cook it, and we'll eat

what we can! Bloody women!"

ELSIE: "But this won't fit in the oven! I don't know why you had to buy such a

big fat bird, in the first place!"

ALF: "Only you is doing the bloody complaining, my dear! Only you is bloody

moaning about the bloody turkey! The good lord has seen fit to bless us with

this turkey!"

ELSIE: "Well, he hasn't got to cook it, has he!"

ALF: "Well, perhaps if you pray a bit harder - he just might come down and

bloody well cook it for you!"

ELSIE: "You pig!"

(Knock on the door)

ALF: "Bloody hell, who's that, bloody knocking? Shouldn't be bloody knocking

on people's houses - not Christmas morning! Tell them to sod off!"

ELSIE: "They're carol singing! Can you hear them?"

ALF: "Yes! Bloody yes! I don't want to bloody well hear them! Bloody annoying

it is! Begging, they are! Bloody parents I blame!"

ELSIE: "What's on the TV?"

ALF: "The same as every bloody Christmas - bloody

garbage! Repeats! Carol

bloody singers, news readers, spitting out the bad news all the bloody time.

Should be illegal, it should!"

ELSIE: "Well, I like the carol singers! I like the fairies, too!"

ALF: "What bloody fairies?"

ELSIE: "The fairies on the tree!"

ALF: "Bloody trees, waste of bloody money! Too much mess on the floor!"

ELSIE: "Well, you don't clean up, do you, I do it! Just like I do all the cooking,

and cleaning, and you go up the pub! Christmas is hard work for me!"

ALF: "Oh...shaddap, you bloody silly moo! Bloody Christmas! Should be banned - too expensive! Bloody three wise men - starting a bloody panic they

did!"

ELSIE: "The hotels are always full at Christmas!"

ALF: "Yeah, poor baby Jesus, was born in a bloody stable! Bloody cold he was,

shivering!"

ELSIE: "Yes, it was terrible! He was born in the stable with them cows and

everything! You see, all the hotels were full! So they couldn't get in one!"

ALF: " You bloody silly moo!!!! They didn't have hotels back then - it wasn't

known as bloody Christmas! Sometimes your intelligence really does bloody

well astound me!"

ELSIE: "I love them carol singers! They sound like they're

happy!"

ALF: "Of course, they're bloody well happy - they going round and annoying

people - singing their bloody heads off - when they should be home with their

mom and dads!"

ELSIE: "Look on the TV, all them stars are on! All working Christmas Day! Even

America has been on!

ALF: "Look?"

Elsie: "I like the America!"

ALF: "The people on the TV are recorded, they don't work on Christmas Day!

There'd be bloody riots if they had to come in to work!"

ELSIE: "But they're there, look, on the TV? How can they be at home - and on our televisions at the same time?"

ALF: "You bloody silly moo! You really are going bloody well senile! Here, have a

bloody drink! They prerecord their shows!"

ELSIE: "Look? Obama's on the TV!"

ALF: "Sod, Obama!!!!"

ELSIE: "Well, I like him! He's got a good suntan!"

ALF: "You bloody silly moo - he's naturally bloody brown! He's running around

bloody well gloating! Bring back yer George Washington!"

ELSIE: "What, Washington? Oh, the pub/bar!"

ALF: "If you listened a bit more to the news - you'd bloody well know which

Washington! It's yer American stuff!"

ELSIE: "Well, I want to see the Queen! When she on?"

ALF: "She's in her bloody palace - having her dinner! She's managed to cook

her bloody turkey! Unlike you! You silly moo!"

ELSIE: " Are you going down the pub tonight?"

ALF: "Yes!"

ELSIE: "You should stay here, with me!"

ALF: "I've got to go! It's traditional!"

ELSIE: "Yes, but it isn't traditional to come back home like a drunken pig!"

ALF: "Shaddap! Stop yer bloody moaning, woman! It's

Christmas! I'll bring yer

a bottle of beer and some nuts back! Ha Ha Ha Ha!!!!"

ELSIE: "You...PIG!!!!

ALF: "Baa bloody humbug!!!!"

THE END

THE BEES AND THE SUNDAY LUNCH

((Old misery guts, Alf Garnett jnr, is back!

The Bees and the Sunday Lunch))

(Note: this script does contain some strong language. In the form of the word BLOODY!)

(Alf jnr is at the dinner table with wife Elsie)

ALF: "What's that?"

ELSIE: "A matchbox!"

ALF: "I know it's a bloody matchbox! What's in it?"

ELSIE: "Bees!"

ALF: "Bees?"

ELSIE: "Yes, bees, don't you listen?"

ALF: "Yes, I do bloody listen, what are you doing with bloody bees?"

ELSIE: "They're for my arthritis!"

ALF: "Arthritis? How do ya mean?"

ELSIE: "Well, if I can get the bees to sting my arthritis they'll kill it?"

ALF: "You bloody silly moo! They don't know where your arthritis is!

ELSIE: "No, but I do!"

ALF: "You really are going bloody senile, you are! Bloody bees! People can fill your head with all sorts of bloody nonsense!"

(Alf's son-in-law, Mike steps in)

MIKE: "Hey, Pops, don't be too hard on Mom - they're only bees! She means no harm!

ALF: "No, but the bloody bees don't know that, do they! Anyway, who rattled your bloody cage? And what's that bloody smelly pong on ya?"

MIKE: "My after shave! Why, what's wrong with it?"

ALF: "You smell like a Peruvian ponse!"

MIKE: "You're only bloody jealous, cos I've got hair - and your just a bloody baldy lookalike!"

ALF: "Shaddap!"

(Alf goes to the pub/bar, and meets his pal Bert for a Sunday drink)

ALF: "Hello Bert? Thought I'd come and annoy ya! Had to get away from the bloody silly moo - keeping bloody bees, she is - going senile too! And that scouse git, who's allergic to bloody work!"

477

BERT: "Hey, Alf, just sniff up and tell me what that smell is?"

ALF: "Smell? What bloody smell?"

BERT: "The smell that fills the air on a Sunday!"

ALF: "What, Beer?"

BERT: "No? Don't be bloody silly! It's roast beef and chicken, with veg and sweet potatoes, and hot gravy. It's what Sunday's were made for, innit?"

ALF: "I don't bother now, Bert! Wife's too ill to cook my lunch. Mind you, I wouldn't mind a roast beef lunch!"

BERT: "I tell you what - why don't you come to my place and stay for lunch? I'm sure the wife will love ya company!"

ALF: "Thanks Bert! You're a very good charitable friend!"

BERT: "Not at all, What are friends for? So its settled!"

ALF: "God bless you Bert, now I can enjoy me beer!"

BERT: "Good! That's settled! I'll fix that one day soon!"

ALF: "Bloody marvellous, innit! I can't even get a Sunday lunch today!"

BERT: "What will you have for your Sunday lunch, Alf?"

ALF: "Beans! Bloody beans, for my Sunday lunch! I can't find the bloody tin opener!"

BERT: "Oh, that's just bad luck, innit!"

ALF: "Yeah, right, no need to bloody well go on! We lost the home help we used to have - bloody council stopped it - government cuts, so they say, Bert!"

BERT: "Well, Alf, got to make tracks - I can smell my roast beef! Come on, Alf, drink up!"

ALF: "Bloody roast beef! And I've got bloody baked beans!!!!"

BERT: "Don't be like that, Alf! It'll soon be Christmas!"

Alf: "Yeah, another bloody Christianity con! Those bloody three wise plonkers! They should be shot for what they started, Bert! Bloody Halloween first, innit!"

BERT: "Oh, I just turn off all the house lights - sod them all!"

ALF: "Ha Ha Ha Ha! Drink up, Bert, happy Sunday to ya! You'd think we were drunk!"

BERT: "I've got news for you...I am bloody drunk!

Alf: "Ha Ha Ha Ha, and you can stuff ya roast bloody beef too!!!!!!!Ha Ha Ha Ha"

THE END

BY DARRYL ASHTON

DEPRESSION AND MENTAL ILLNESS

The path of light just
seems so far away,
All I want is to go and
feel okay.
The tunnel is all dark -
and nothing is bright,
When will I ever feel
completely alright?

My spirit is in torment -
that is for sure,
I just want the pain to
ease - and find the cure.
The enemy within - I
know is a pest,
It tests my loyalty - I
put it to the test.

The road to happiness

seems so long,

Sometimes I feel like

life is so wrong!

No one sees the inner

self,

As you always feel like

you're left on the shelf.

Depression is there -

but no one can see it -

Until the time comes -

and you have a fit?

Mental illness is so

little known,

I wish I was home in

my home-grown dome.

Being happy every day -

and always a smile -

But really deep down -

I will run a mile!

Nowhere to call home -

no one does care,

Why do people just

gloat and stare?

Is there a bright light

for me to see?

Is it deep within the

sea?

The lord has the answer,

I know that's true,

Is this the end of me

and you?

I see a shadow of light

ahead,

I can now go - and rest

my head.

Just to be rid of this

mental-health issue,

To go to sleep - oh, I

will miss you.

Bless me father - my soul

does come,

Up to heaven - in heaven

to roam.

The land I leave - is all

make believe,

My soul wants out - it has

to leave.

The future is bright - I now

see the sign,

I go now to sleep - the bells

do chime.

May the good lord have

mercy upon my soul,

As now, my friends, I hear

the call.

Goodbye to depression I

say that so true,

For heaven is where my

life is so new.

My one way ticket to peace

and love,

I now join my God - in

heaven, above.

BY DARRYL ASHTON

THE BEDROOM TAX

See the politician's vote,
the bedroom tax will
stay,
I'd better get my hat and
coat, because I'm not
going to pay.

Damn the Tory's, damn
the Lib Dems, damn the
Labour few,
They are all the same to
me, one politician's view.

Whilst the country wiles
away, another forced
decree,
I am going to have my

say, I hope my speech is

free.

People laying down the

law, Eton educates,

Oxford bags another war,

whilst Cambridge just

dictates.

These toffee nosed posh

bleeders, a title for their

home,

The Parliamentary leaders,

must think that they're in

Rome.

A House of little Caesars,

getting rich on us.

They claim for their

Maltesers, so minimum

the fuss.

A land for every beggar,

who cares to hit our

shores,

Rewards for them are

mega, they love the

House of Lords.

A gang of old mad cronies,

voting with their stick,

A has-been load of phonies,

making me feel sick.

Where the hell is Blighty,

the spirit we once knew?

We used to be almighty,

now we are just the few.

The bedroom tax is unfair,

but politician's fiddle,

They'll even sing and dance

all night, shouting; "hey,

diddle diddle!"

I see the politician's vote,

the bedroom tax is dead,

It really is an unfair tax,

let's put this tax to bed!

BY DARRYL ASHTON

WELCOME TO COALITION AIRWAYS

(After being treated to a flight on Air Force One recently, the Prime Minister could be tempted to order his own official plane. But he'd have to work hard to get the Lib Dems on board. So what might a flight on Coalition Airways be like?)

Good morning, ladies and gentlemen, not forgetting members of the Gay, Lesbian, Bisexual and Transgender community. This is Captain Cameron speaking, but you can call me Dave.

Please allow me to apologise for the lengthy delay in our boarding process, caused by unforeseen technical glitches with our state-of-the-art automated retina recognition scheme and the arrest of several passengers for alleged racist remarks while passing through security.

We also apologise for any inconvenience caused by our new seating allocation system, which is based on proportional representation and is designed to ensure equality of access to all sections of the aircraft.

I am also very proud to announce that in keeping with our

fairness agenda, passengers earning less than £10,000 a year fly free on Coalition Airways. This is being paid for by a 50 per cent surcharge on passengers in Tycoon Class.

Flying duties today are being shared between the Captain and Co-Pilot Clegg. Please don't be alarmed if the aircraft experiences sudden changes in direction. Your safety and your comfort is our number one priority.

Would all passengers being extradited to America please keep their handcuffs and shackles fastened at all times and remember to wear the special orange sleep-suits provided.

Passengers fitted with electronic ankle tags are asked to switch them off for take-off and landing as they could interfere with our navigation equipment.

Our purser, Mr Osborne, will be passing among you collecting airline duty, carbon taxes, mansion taxes and VAT at 20 per cent. In our efforts to keep costs down, we regret to announce that full-fare passengers in the higher-rate tax bracket are not entitled to free children's meals.

Alcoholic beverages will be available, priced at a minimum 50p per unit ABV. Sales of intoxicating drinks will be tightly restricted to prevent anyone going berserk in the Strangers Cabin and head – butting other passengers.

I would like to take this opportunity to welcome aboard those couples embarking on same-sex honeymoons. They will receive unlimited complimentary champagne for the duration of our flight. Cabin crew will also be distributing landing cards, which must be completed in full. I would remind you that the terms 'husband', 'wife', 'mother' and 'father' are now illegal and should not be used on any official documentation. The correct term is either 'partner/spouse' or 'progenitor'. Failure to comply will result in arrest by our air-marshals, a fine of £10,000 and six months in prison.

Those of you planning to connect to onward flights to Scotland will have to complete separate customs and immigration forms and produce your passport at border control. We do hope all the passengers enjoy our in-flight meal service, which is being freshly prepared in the galley on the top-of-the-range barbecue presented to the Captain on his recent visit to America.

We try to source as much as possible from reputable British companies. All the crockery in Tycoon Class has been supplied by Royal Doulton, from its factories in Indonesia, and our cutlery is forged from the finest Sheffield steel, in India.

It is also our policy to feature a selection of traditional British dishes. Today we are offering a vegetable lasagne, prepared by the gourmet chef Ed Balls-Cooper in his subsidised second home kitchen. Unfortunately, the steak and kidney is not available, as Mr Pickles, the chief steward in our Community Class cabin, ate all the pies.

We also pride ourselves on the stringent security measures taken for your safety and convenience. In the unlikely event of you spotting a fellow passenger trying to explode his underpants, please alert a member of the cabin crew. There is no cause for alarm. It may simply be a case of mid-air turbulence caused by Chef Balls-Cooper's vegetable lasagne.

The hacking of mobile phones in flight is not permitted. Smoking is strictly forbidden anywhere on the aircraft, including the washrooms. Dogging and cottaging are allowed, once we are airborne, but we would kindly request that no more than four passengers use a single washroom at the same time.

Given the need for budgetary restraint, this aircraft has been designed to perform a joint civilian and military role. Consequently, we will be diverting via Syria to bomb Damascus and descending to 3,000 feet to allow members of our special forces to deploy their parachutes.

During this time, we may experience some anti-aircraft fire, so all passengers will be asked to fasten their seat belts and assume the brace position. Ladies and gentlemen, I do apologise for the continuing delay. I have just heard from our ground crew that our flight today will have to be postponed.

Even if we do manage to get airborne, there is a possibility that Co-Pilot Clegg and several members of the cabin crew will abandon the aircraft and parachute to earth in an attempt to save themselves, in clear breach of both health and safety guidelines and the Coalition Airways Agreement.

So I'm afraid I must ask you to deplane in an orderly fashion and take all your belongings and rubbish with you. As part of our ongoing commitment to combating climate change, we intend to empty the bins on this aircraft only once a fortnight.

Thank you for choosing Coalition Airways. Normal service will be resumed in 2015.

Here endeth the flight.

THE END

BY DARRYL ASHTON

FAWLTY TOWERS...THE RETURN!!!!

(I say, Fawlty, there are men wearing frocks in the cocktail bar!)

(The following is my own take on how Fawlty Towers would be like if it was recommissioned under present-day diversity and equality guidelines...)

FAWLTY: "Morning, Major."

MAJOR: "Papers here yet, Fawlty?"

FAWLTY: "Absolutely, Major. Ever since that wonderful Indian family took over the newsagents they're on the doorstep at 5am prompt, rain or shine. They can teach the bone-idle British a thing or two, eh?"

MAJOR: "Indian, you say? I knew a girl once. I must have been keen on her because I took her to see India."

FAWLTY: "At the Oval?"

MAJOR: "No, India. Wonderful country, charming people. Industrious, honest as the day is long, marvellous cooks. More billionaires than you can shake a stick at. Got their own space programme, too.

FAWLTY: "Jewel in the Crown, Major. I'm thinking of turning Fawlty Towers into a sort of Best Exotic Marigold

Hotel in reverse, somewhere sophisticated Indians can come to relax on the English Riviera.

MAJOR: " Didn't think you could stand foreigners, Fawlty?"

FAWLTY: " Au contraire, Major. Can't get enough of them. A few Indian billionaires might raise the tone of this place, not like the usual riff-raff we get in here.

MAJOR: " Riff-raff?"

FAWLTY: " Torbay Conservative Association, Women's Institute; Countryside Alliance..."

MAJOR: " Remember when we had Mrs Thatcher down here to address the Conservative Association dinner?"

FAWLTY: " Don't mention that scabby old bat to me. Damage she did to Britain. My heart still bleeds for the miners. She was completely mad, you know. Complained about the view from her room."

MAJOR: " The view?"

FAWLTY: " What do you expect to see from a Torquay hotel window: Sydney Opera House? The Hanging Gardens of Babylon? Herds of wildebeest sweeping majestically...? No, she said, I expect to see British fishing boats, catching British fish in British waters, not a flotilla of Spanish factory ships. If it's British ships you want to see, I said, you'd better book into a hotel in the bloody Maldives, you fascist, imperialistic cow."

MAJOR: " Maldives? In Worcestershire?"

FAWLTY: " No, Major. That what our Argentinian cousins call the Falkland Islands. We should hand them over tomorrow if you ask me. I don't know what we're doing in the South Atlantic, or Afghanistan for that matter."

MAJOR: " But I thought you were a fan of Mrs Thatcher, Fawlty. You used to have a picture of her in reception, next to the moose's head."

FAWLTY: " That was Sybil's idea, Major. Worshipped the woman. God knows why..."

(Enter Sybil through the front door)

SYBIL: " Baaa-zzzil!!!"

FAWLTY: " Hello, my little iron Lady. We were just..."

SYBIL: " Why are all those caravans cluttering up the car park, Basil?"

FAWLTY: " I'm glad you asked that, dear. I've agreed that the travelling community can use the car park as a temporary campsite until they can find an alternative to Dale Farm."

SYBIL: " I want them gone now, Basil. There's nowhere for the guests to park."

FAWLTY: " But we can't evict them. They are a vulnerable minority who suffer terrible discrimination and deprivation. And anyway, they've agreed to Tarmac the drive for nothing."

SYBIL: " Mr O'Reilly was supposed to have Tarmacked the drive weeks ago, Basil. Why didn't you use those nice Polish builders? What's he been doing?"

FAWLTY: " He's been refurbishing the multi-faith prayer room, dear. We've got a group from Finsbury Park Mosque arriving at the weekend and they want the all-you-can-eat halal buffet facing Mecca."

SYBIL: " And I thought I told you to ring the council and get them to empty dustbins. They haven't been round for weeks."

FAWLTY: " It's not their fault, Sybil, it's the savage cuts being imposed by local councils by the Bullingdon Club Coalition Government.

SYBIL: " I'll be imposing some savage cuts on you, Basil, if those dustbins aren't emptied by tonight. We've got a gay wedding reception tomorrow and I don't want a repeat of that business with the rat.

(Phone rings)

SYBIL: " Fawlty Towers reception, how can I help you? Of course, Mr Jackson, right away. I'll get my husband to attend to it immediately. Basil, the American couple in Room 109 are still having problems with the air conditioning."

FAWLTY: " Pah! Typical Americans. Look, whatever you do, don't mention the illegal war in Iraq. I mentioned it once, but I think I got away with it. Still, that's Republicans for you."

SYBIL: " Basil, I don't think they are Republicans. They're African-Americans, from the Martin Luther King Foundation, over here for a conference on reparations for slavery."

FAWLTY: " Oh, African-Americans. Why didn't you say so? I'll get straight on to it, my Little Englander."

SYBIL: " You are a pathetic specimen, Basil. And when you've done that, I want you to get on to Mr Clegg about his Britain In Europe meeting in the Mandelson Suite. Tell him the room has been closed for fumigation and won't be available again until 2017. And then ring Mr Farage at the Red Lion and tell him the same thing."

(Exit Sybil)

MAJOR: " Does that mean the UKIP dinner is off tonight, Fawlty?"

FAWLTY: " Fraid so, Major. Don't tell Sybil, but I've already called Farage and refunded his deposit. Whatever you think of that privileged and toffy-nosed Cameron, he says he was right about UKIP. Bunch of fruit-cakes, loonies and closet racists in blazers."

MAJOR: " No, no, no, Fawlty, I won't accept that! They're going to be the next government? And nearly all of the UK, say that, Fawlty?"

FAWLTY: " Of course, they are, Major, drunken old sod!"

Major: " Wearing blazers, Fawlty?"

FAWLTY: " Yes, Major, blazers. I've been meaning to have a word with you about our new dress code."

MAJOR: " Dress code? Don't tell me you're lifting the ban on ladies wearing trousers in the cocktail bar?"

FAWLTY: " No. I'm lifting the ban on men wearing dresses in the cocktail bar.

Fawlty Towers is becoming Torquay's first Trans-Friendly hotel."

MAJOR: " Trans-what, Fawlty?"

FAWLTY: " Transgendered, trans-sexual, transvestite... call them what you will, Major?"

MAJOR: " Oh, I see. Ladyboys! When I was in Brazil..."

FAWLTY: " Keep your voice down, Major. We've got the local LGBT committee having lunch in the Burchill Room today. Chef's running them up a nice Waldorf Salad."

MAJOR: " Where's Manuel, Fawlty? Haven't seen him for

ages.

FAWLTY: " He's gone back to Barcelona. Never got over that business with his granddaughter - or the death of his pet rat!"

MAJOR: " What business?"

FAWLTY: " That phone call from Russell Brand and Jonathan Ross. You know; Mr Brand who always looks as if he needs a good wash, a haircut, and a shave?"

MAJOR: " Oh, yes, I read about it. Shocking, quite shocking. Now I remember what I came down here for. Papers here yet, Fawlty?"

FAWLTY: " Just some paper called The Blackpool Gazette, Major!"

MAJOR: " Oh, no thanks, total rubbish, Fawlty."

FAWLTY: " Quite!"

THE END

WRITTEN BY DARRYL ASHTON

WELCOME TO A HEAVENLY PARADISE...
THE WELCOMING HOME OF GOD.

I approach the gates of

heaven - I see God

standing there,

He smiles at me so

warmly - he really does

so care.

The scene is so surreal,

the angels are smiling

too -

But the place is really

so quiet - there's never

any queue.

I check in at the pearly

gates - a man with a

long, long white beard,

He asks me very friendly;

'are you feeling tired?'

He gives me a hug and

I start to cry - as this is

now my home -

I am now in club paradise -

where I'm free to roam!

I look on down from

in the fountain - I see

my family all crying;

'But God tells me they

will all live on - and start

a new beginning?'

God takes me by the

hand - and he smiles

so bright at me,

He then pats me on

the shoulder - and all I

feel is glee.

So now I am in heaven -
there isn't any more
pain,
I can just sit down all
peacefully - and watch
the clouds make rain.
I am at peace - this is
true - I'm in a heavenly
place,
But please don't mourn
too long for me - I really
do feel ace?

You won't believe the
sights I see - it really
is a dream,
We all sit and dine

together - and even eat

ice cream!!

The magic of the new

kingdom - is always

open to you,

Always believe in the

miracle of heaven - it

happens to be...TRUE!

BY DARRYL ASHTON

THE MAGIC OF AMERICA

America, America, you
really are so great,
The home of Hollywood
movies - acting talent
you did create.
America is so vast - and
every state can tell a
story;
'Here's something from
me - in poetic glory.'

America is the home
of Hollywood and more,
All them action heroes -
that we all adore.
Even the musicals -
where they danced

the days away,

From tap-dancing - to

big band sounds - and

singers all did sway.

Even the gangsters - oh

they really were so mean,

James Cagney to Humphrey

Bogart - and more in

between.

Even Elliott Ness, was

chasing lots of troubles;

'Especially trying catch

Al Capone - and his

gun-tooting' Untouchables!'

Gene Kelly and Donald O'

Connor - their tap dancing

was pristine -

Even when they were

dancing too - 'Singin' In

The Rain'.

All kinds of musicals were

so majestically made,

From Showboat to Carousel,

their magic didn't fade.

The singers too were superb,

they sang of rock n roll,

Every kind of singer hit their

charts - even music hall!

From Frankie Laine to Guy

Mitchell - and Andy Williams too.

Even the king of rock n roll -

Elvis Presley - they were the

privileged few.

There are also lots of others -

who made America great,

But there's just far too many -

for me to appreciate.

Big band sounds - and soft

melodies -

All this fabulous music -

American golden oldies!

America, America, we thank

you for your talent,

From every state on your map -

each a gigantic giant.

God Bless America - and all

the talent there,

Hollywood and Paramount -

and Walt Disney, all are very

rare.

BY DARRYL ASHTON

Made in the USA
Charleston, SC
29 May 2016